Dr. Seuss & Co. Go to War

Dr. Seuss & Co. Go to War

*The World War II Editorial Cartoons of
America's Leading Comic Artists*

André Schiffrin

PUBLISHED IN COOPERATION WITH THE DR. SEUSS COLLECTION
AT THE UNIVERSITY OF CALIFORNIA, SAN DIEGO

THE NEW PRESS

NEW YORK
LONDON

Requests for permission to reproduce selections from this book should be mailed to:
Permissions Department, The New Press, 38 Greene Street, New York, NY 10013.

Published in the United States by The New Press, New York, 2009
Distributed by Perseus Distribution

LIBRARY OF CONGRESS CATALOGING-IN-PUBLICATION DATA
Schiffrin, André.
Dr. Seuss & Co. go to war : the World War II editorial cartoons of
America's leading comic artists / André Schiffrin.
p. cm.
Cartoons drawn for the New York daily newspaper *PM*.
Companion and sequel to *Dr. Seuss Goes to War*.
Includes bibliographical references and index.
ISBN 978-1-59558-470-0 (alk. paper)
1. World War, 1939–945—Caricatures and cartoons. 2. World
politics—1900–1945—Caricatures and cartoons. 3. United States—Politics
and government—1933–945—Caricatures and cartoons. 4. Editorial
cartoons—United States—History--20th century. 5. American wit and humor,
Pictorial. I. Geisel, Theodor Seuss, 1904–1991. Dr. Seuss goes to war. II.
PM (New York, N.Y. : Daily ed.) III. Title. IV. Title: Dr. Seuss and Company
go to war.
D745.2.S25 2009
940.5302'07—dc22
2009024967

The New Press was established in 1990 as a not-for-profit alternative to the large, commercial publishing houses currently dominating the book publishing industry. The New Press operates in the public interest rather than for private gain, and is committed to publishing, in innovative ways, works of educational, cultural, and community value that are often deemed insufficiently profitable.

www.thenewpress.com

Book design and Composition by Lovedog Studio
This book was set in Fairfield Light

Printed in the United States of America

2 4 6 8 10 9 7 5 3 1

Contents

Dr. Seuss & Co. Go to War

Introduction

This book is both a companion and a sequel to *Dr. Seuss Goes to War*, by Richard H. Minear. Published a decade ago, *Dr. Seuss Goes to War* introduced the contemporary reader to Theodor Geisel's forgotten career as a political cartoonist, as Dr. Seuss. From 1940 until he joined the army in January 1943, Geisel drew some four hundred cartoons for

the short-lived but exciting progressive New York tabloid *PM*. Minear's book, which featured two hundred images, was an enormous success, selling more than 100,000 copies. For the generations that knew Geisel only for his children's books, this was a revelation.

But Dr. Seuss, the name signed to Geisel's cartoons, was only one of a number of distinguished illustrators who worked for *PM*. The purpose of this collection is not only to publish more than a hundred of the cartoons that Minear could not include but also to publish the hundreds by others, which together give us a remarkable look at the issues, domestic and international, facing progressive Americans during the years of World War II.

I have tried to avoid duplication with *Dr. Seuss Goes to War* but have included a few cartoons on which I needed to comment specifically. This volume will offer a broader look at the issues about which Dr. Seuss drew, as well as those that developed after he left *PM*. I will give an analysis of the issues that all the cartoonists dealt with, using not only the articles and editorials in *PM* but also the views of subsequent historians. A certain number of references will be unfamiliar to the contemporary reader and will be explained. Others need to be contextualized. However, a great many of the cartoons seem to me self-explanatory, so I have left them without comment.

PM published literally thousands of nonpolitical cartoons and illustrations during its brief life, 1940–1948. Many were similar to those appearing in the *New Yorker, Collier's,* the *Saturday Evening Post, Esquire*, and other popular magazines of the day. Indeed, many of those who contributed to PM worked at the same time with these very magazines. I have not included these purely humorous cartoons, along with much of the illustrative work that appeared in PM, since they were not directly related to the war or to the key political issues.

The images included in these pages are those that express editorial views, those of the artists themselves and often those of the newspaper. These cartoons usually appeared on the editorial page, sometimes illustrating directly PM's views. Together they give an excellent picture of the evolution of the war, at home and abroad.

The Cartoonists in This Volume

Many of those who drew for PM went on to become famous in other media. A few had already established reputations, largely from their work in the radical American and European press, in journals such as the *New Masses*. In some cases, PM was the bridge between these and the more popular American media. In other cases, their work had already appeared in the *New Yorker* and elsewhere, though their PM work was usually far more political.

Perhaps the most striking discovery in these pages is the PM cartoons of the great American artist Saul Steinberg. He drew some fifty illustrations in its pages, both as a kind of comic strip and as political cartoons.

To my knowledge, these have never been included in the many collections of his works and go unmentioned in the encyclopedia articles about him and in the biography published by his Steinberg Foundation. Born in Rumania in 1914, he moved to study in Italy, his work having already been strongly influenced by the drawings of its futurists. The adoption of the Italian Fascist government's anti-Jewish law in 1941 led him to flee to Santo Domingo, where he awaited the visa that would allow him to come to the United States. But his first images appeared in *Life* as early as 1940 and even while awaiting entry into the United States, he began contributing cartoons to the *New Yorker*, which sponsored his visa to the United States. Ultimately he would contribute a total of 1,200 pictures as well as ninety *New Yorker* covers, including his iconic image of America seen from New York.

On the day that he became an American citizen, according to his obituary in the *New York Times*, he was sent to China to work with guerrilla forces, teaching them to blow up bridges. The head of the OSS (the agency in charge of espionage and sabotage before the CIA), William Donovan, must have thought this a waste of his talents. He was transferred to North Africa and then Italy, to draw cartoons that were meant to arouse anti-Nazi feeling in Germany. These were dropped behind enemy lines and included in the OSS-published newspaper *Neues Deutschland* (a title that was ironically kept by the East Germans as the name of one of their leading newspapers).

Steinberg's sketches of his time in the military in China, India, and elsewhere were published in the *New Yorker* and later, in 1945, in a collection called *All in Line*. Some of the anti-Nazi cartoons may well have echoed his work in *PM* (or may indeed be identical to his OSS work; not having access to the OSS newspaper, we can only guess).

Other of *PM*'s cartoonists would have long, flourishing careers in the *New Yorker*, and, like Steinberg, many of them were born in Europe. Mischa Richter, one of *PM*'s most frequent contributors, was born in Kharkov, Russia, in 1912. He came to the United States as a youngster of eleven and was so promising that he immediately got a scholarship to the Boston Museum of Fine Arts school and subsequently one at Yale School of Fine Arts. Afterward, he worked for the WPA and the *New Masses*, a radical magazine.

Another *PM* contributor was Carl Rose, whose 1930 *New Yorker* cartoons already had a political touch (though he is best remembered for his classic image of a child saying "I say it's spinach and I say the hell with it"). His work also appeared in *Esquire* and later in *Penthouse*. Like Dr. Seuss, he was one of the first cartoonists to run in *PM*.

Leo Hershfield joined *PM* as a staff artist and, in addition to cartoons, provided many of its most ambitious portfolios of illustrations, one of full-page pictures of wartime leaders, another of life in wartime Washington, as well as many spot illustrations. *PM* was founded with the assumptions that it would use photos, maps, and illustrations extensively. Its weekend section was called the *Picture Magazine*, where many of Hershfield's images appeared (though they are not included in this volume).

Al Hirschfeld also contributed to *PM* before becoming famous over the years for his theatrical cartoons in the *New York Times*. For over seventy years, he covered every Broadway opening night. Hirschfeld began drawing political cartoons even before *PM* appeared, publishing as early as 1933 some strongly anti-Hitler work.

Two of *PM*'s most prolific cartoonists were Melville Bernstein and Eric Godal. They became *PM*'s most frequent contributors after Seuss, appearing usually on the editorial page. Godal was another European immigrant, born in Germany in 1899. His series of cartoons on everyday life in Germany was therefore particularly acute, though he became known later for a very successful group of children's books. Bernstein and Godal's joint contributions are so numerous, even more so than Dr. Seuss's, that I have been able to reproduce only a relatively small portion of their cartoons from *PM*.

Two other cartoonists were better known for their work as artists: John Groth (born in 1908) for his pastels and drawings about the experience of World War II, and Louis Raemaekers (born in Holland in 1869), who was best known for his cartoons about World War I, which *PM* proudly republished.

Daniel Fitzpatrick's political cartoons became nationally famous during the 1950s, when his work for the *St. Louis Post-Dispatch* was nationally syndicated. He was their editorial cartoonist for most of his life, but he also contributed a number of cartoons to *PM*, several of which are included here.

Arthur Szyk was one of the first cartoonists to invoke the Holocaust. Born in Poland, he came to the United States in 1940 and was one of the most influential artists for his detailed and damning drawings of the Axis leaders. He painted covers for *Time* magazine and appeared in many mainstream publications as well as *PM*. His cartoons in the *New York Post* (on July 20, 1943) and in *PM* invoked the Holocaust before many others. He was involved in the work of those around Peter Bergson, the militant anti-Holocaust lobbyist, whose organization was the major group trying to force American public opinion to pressure the government to save the Jews. (More on this in the section on *PM* and the Holocaust below.) In recent years, several major exhibits have been devoted to his work, one in Berlin in 2008 and several others at the Holocaust Museum in Washington, DC. The exhibit in 2002 was accompanied by a lavish full-color catalog.

The Cartoonists Not in This Book

The cartoons published by *PM* were so numerous, literally thousands in number, that it would take a dozen volumes to reproduce them all. Many were very funny but unrelated to the war, beyond the classic jokes about servicemen and their girlfriends or housewives coping with rationing. These cartoons were exactly what appeared in the rest of the press and, while often the work of some of the period's best cartoonists, did not make sense for this volume. However it is impressive to see that *PM* published the work of Chon Day, Don Freeman, Virgil Partch, and Gardner Rea, many of whose cartoons can be seen in the *New Yorker* collections published over the years. *PM* also published full-page collections, called *War Bores* or *War Relief*, which were largely the work of Charles Martin. James Thurber also contributed a column, called *If You Ask Me*, in 1940, which was illustrated with his famous sketches and cartoons, but, as one would expect, had no political content.

Finally, *PM* ran a number of series that were more artistic in nature. In addition to Leo Hirschfield's impressive portraits, the newspaper ran many drawings by Reginald Marsh as well as a series of images by Grant Reynard on everyday life in New York during the war years. These marvelous drawings, reminiscent of John Sloan's earlier sketches of New York, deserve to be published by themselves, but, again, did not fit within the limits of this book.

Though at first *PM* refused to run comic strips, a standard part of most newspapers, it did finally give in. Its first attempt, in August 1941, was a humorous series called *Patoruzu*, featuring a stereotyped American Indian, which would probably embarrass today's readers. In December 1941 it launched *Vic Jordan*, a series resembling Milt Caniff's famous *Terry and the Pirates* and sharing its wartime patriotism. In 1942, *PM* added *Barnaby*, which became by far its most enduring contribution. Crockett Johnson's creation of a child and his imagined companion became an enormous success and resulted in many books over the years.

It is striking that *PM*, which devoted so many pages to public service information, clearly felt that purveying humor at a time of war was in itself a public service. It imposed no political line on its cartoonists. Those who wished to express their political views were free to do so and some, clearly, were hired with that in mind. But thousands of other cartoons appeared, as they did in the national magazines, just to give their readers a laugh. (There's another aspect that's worth mentioning: for most of its life, *PM* refused advertising, so cartoons and photographs broke up what would otherwise have been solid pages of print.)

The Organization of this Volume

As was the case with *Dr. Seuss Goes to War*, the cartoons here are organized by subject and then chronologically within the categories. (There are a few exceptions where, in order to group one artist's work, I have made minor changes in the sequence of images.)

We start in June 1940, the week France fell to the Germans, when the paper was born. For America this was the period leading up to the war, and in *PM* was when Dr. Seuss's images predominated. Then we have the cartoons about the home front, again with many of the Seuss cartoons that did not appear in *Dr. Seuss Goes to War*. After that, the cartoons about the major enemies, Hitler's Germany and Japan, starting before the war and continuing on to 1943, when the tide turned. Then a section on Hitler's foreign allies, primarily Mussolini, but also Franco, Vichy France, and others. Finally a section on the decline of Axis power, which I date from the end of the battle of Stalingrad in early 1943 until the end of the war and Hiroshima.

Each section is preceded by a short text, explaining the more difficult references, some of which may seem incomprehensible to today's readers. (Who today remembers the Japanese threat to the island of Madagascar? What Japanese threat?!) Whenever possible, I have done this syncretically, drawing both from comments in *PM* and analysis from contemporary historians.

The Beginnings of *PM*

The origins of *PM*, New York's newest and most radical newspaper in 1940, were very unlikely. The paper was the brainchild of Ralph Ingersoll, a Yale graduate close to New York's high society and formerly the number two to Henry Luce, the archconservative publisher of *Time*, *Life*, and *Fortune*.

It was Ingersoll's society connections that had led the *New Yorker*'s legendary editor, Harold Ross, to hire him. Ross wanted him to work on the magazine's new Talk of the Town section and Ingersoll duly visited nightclubs and parties. By 1929, Ingersoll had had enough of Ross's bullying and left, to be hired by Henry Luce as the editor of his new monthly, *Fortune*, aimed at big business and high finance. He was extremely successful editing this new publication, in spite of running articles favorable to the New Deal and hiring such antiestablishment figures as the radical journalist Dwight MacDonald and the photographer Walker Evans. Ingersoll then went on to *Time* magazine, which, under Luce, was a determinedly reactionary paper, anti–New Deal, anti-labor, and pro-Franco. Luce insisted that every story embody his ideas, and the editors were notorious for discarding the reporter's copy to run something closer to the boss's taste. In retrospect, one can see *Time* as the anti-*PM*, a paper that embodied all the values that Ingersoll wanted to purge from his experience and from the press in general. Before leaving, however, he went on to *Life*, where again he was so successful that Luce offered him a totally unprecedented million dollars to stay on for another five years, more than ten million in today's money.

But Ingersoll had had enough of Luce and his values and set out to raise the money to launch his own paper, money that would be even more crucial because Ingersoll was determined not to run ads. His early editor Penn Kimball was quoted as remembering a comment by David Lawrence, then editor of the new *U.S. News*. Lawrence had "once said a friendly word about the New Deal and lost 25 advertising clients."[1]

Ingersoll doubted that the ads would actually pay for themselves. But, since *PM* would be fiercely on the left, he was also determined to have total independence and to be free of such pressures. In his opening statement about the paper's aims, he said that the paper "should stand for the publisher's conception of a better world."[2] This, he famously stated, would be a paper "against people who push other people around . . . we propose to applaud those who seek constructively to improve the way men live together. We are American and we prefer democracy to any other form of government. . . . The Fascist philosophy represents a live threat to everything we believe in." In Ingersoll's somewhat prolix style (his internal memos were notorious for their length), we see the main lines of the future *PM*, pro–New Deal, pro-labor and, in 1940, pro-intervention, that is, in favor of helping England against Hitler.

PM would be very much a minority voice in the New York press. With the exception of the *New York Post*, the main papers were powerful and conservative to reactionary. In 1939, the *New York Times* had a circulation of 475,000 daily and an impressive 800,000 on Sundays. It was very Republican in its stance, anti-Roosevelt in the 1940 elections, anti-labor, though pro-British.

The other "respectable" morning broadsheet, the *Herald Tribune*, was to its right, with a daily sale of 350,000 and 525,000 on Sundays. Again, it was anti-labor and against FDR, though, like the *Times*, pro-intervention. The other major dailies were shriller in their politics, the *Sun* with a daily circulation of 300,000 and the *Journal American* with 600,000 daily and a million on Sunday shared Hearst's anti-communist obsessions with its tabloid partner, the *Daily Mirror*, which had a daily sale of 800,000 and 1,500,000 on Sundays. William Randolph Hearst's papers were a major chain throughout the country and, along with Colonel McCormick's *Chicago Tribune*, were at the vanguard of reactionary and isolationist papers.

The other leading tabloid, the *Daily News* (like the *Daily Mirror* charging two cents as opposed to three for the broadsheets) had a daily circulation of 1.9 million and 3.4 million on Sundays, partly because of its many comics. Though these outnumbered the news pages, what coverage they ran was strongly isolationist. The *World Telegram* with 410,000 daily ran the ultrareactionary Westbrook Pegler and was staunchly anti-FDR, though pro-Allies.

On the left, the tabloid *New York Post* had 235,000 readers and was liberally Democratic. The *Post* had been bought in 1933 by David Stern, whose *Philadelphia Record* was the only liberal voice among that city's ten papers. He hired I.F. Stone to write editorials, though the two broke up over Stone's backing of the popular front in 1939. The paper was then bought by George Backer, who kept it running for many years. While Stone in the *Post* had opposed the Hitler-Stalin pact in 1940, the *Daily Worker* was totally faithful to the Communist Party line, strongly antiwar, voicing many of the arguments of the right-wing isolationists.

PM was launched in a city with eight major dailies (plus one in Brooklyn, the *Eagle*) and a panoply of foreign-language papers, far more than exist in today's press-challenged New York, which has only three local dailies. Ingersoll hoped to reach a million readers and even dreamt of doubling the *Daily News'* circulation, a wildly optimistic assumption. He started the paper with a massive publicity campaign so effective that readers stormed the delivery trucks before they could even reach the newsstands, and all 400,000 of its first run were sold out, at the end selling for ten times the high cover price of five cents. But their curiosity satisfied, the readers did not stay. Circulation fell from 350,000, which would have been very healthy, to 40,000 in a few weeks. Partly due to the paper's chaotic internal organization, the list of subscribers, which had been gathered in an expensive prepublication drive, was lost (though some staffers suspected sabotage).

The paper faced massive opposition from the *Daily News*, which told newsstand owners that they could either sell the *News* or *PM*. Ingersoll intervened with Mayor LaGuardia, who suggested he buy separate display cases alongside the stands, but that did not help his sales outside the city. (The other papers would eventually block *PM*'s access to the AP newswire as well.)

By August 1940, circulation had fallen to 31,000 and the paper was facing bankruptcy. Marshall Field, the liberal Chicago millionaire, offered to buy all the shares at 20 percent of the price that had been paid for them, and the other stockholders were relieved to agree. Field would own the paper until the end. He would lose four million dollars supporting *PM,* even though the paper managed to sell more than 150,000 copies for much of the war. The one exception was during the New York newspaper strike of 1944 when *PM* alone appeared and was eagerly snatched up by 500,000 purchasers. Unfortunately they did not stay with the paper afterward.

After the war, Field and Ingersoll fought over the question of adding advertising, which Field deemed necessary, and in 1946 (after an absence during part of the war) Ingersoll quit in protest (though there were many signs by then of his dissatisfaction with *PM*). The paper would continue under Field's ownership until 1948, when it was sold to Bartley Crum and Joseph Barnes, who had written for *PM*. It was renamed the *Star.* It added many promising new names and was the only New York paper to back Truman's 1948 bid (even the *Post* felt it was a hopeless campaign). But all

these efforts were in vain, and on January 28, 1949, the paper died, all attempts to raise new capital and recruit new readers having failed. A final attempt at reincarnation, as the *Compass*, would last only a year. By then the climate of the cold war had fatally diminished even *PM*'s relatively small progressive audience.

No one seemed sure why *PM*'s initial sales should have declined so abruptly. The paper looked good; it was well designed, influenced by Ingersoll's work at *Time* and *Life*. This experience also led him to make extensive use of photographs, maps, and illustrations, not to mention the cartoons in this collection. He ran many of the famous photographs of the city by Helen Levitt as well as Weegee's dark picture of the city's underside. Margaret Bourke-White was among the many other photographers *PM* used as well.

Ingersoll was able to recruit a remarkable staff: some ten thousand applied for the two hundred well-paid jobs on the paper. In addition, he recruited some of the country's leading writers as commentators: Dashiell Hammett, Lillian Hellman, Edmund Wilson, and Malcolm Cowley. Young Dr. Spock was brought in to follow the life of Baby Lois, born on the same day as the newspaper, for her first two years. But somehow, all of this did not suffice. Indeed, some of these names, such as Hammett and Hellman, led to accusations of communism and Moscow gold (though the investors were bona fide American millionaires). Ingersoll was certainly willing to hire Communists and even asked Earl Browder, the party head, to send over a reporter to represent the party's views. (He quit shortly thereafter.) Ingersoll felt that he wanted to hear all sides of a question and make the final decisions (which sounds vaguely familiar in the first days of the Obama presidency), but he did not realize that the divisions in the Newspaper Guild, *PM*'s trade union, would lead to endless factional fights and eventual accusations by some of the anticommunists, like James Wechsler, that the paper had been controlled by the Communist Party. At the same time, to prove you can't please everybody, Browder would complain to Eleanor Roosevelt, a great *PM* fan, about the "Trotskyites" who'd taken control of the paper.

When *PM* was launched, Ingersoll thought labor issues would be the most important. In addition, the paper began with a series of investigations in consumer fraud, exposing the city's butchers who injected water into their meat, so as to charge higher prices, and the like. Clearly he hoped to reach a popular, even working-class audience. Many of the paper's columns featured advice to the housewife. There was a daily résumé of the sales advertised in the other papers, which even brought a fan letter from a Macy's executive. But these frills failed to lure the readers of the city's tabloids, with their gossip, sports coverage, and comics.

In any case, the war, rather than the day-to-day issues, soon became the major question. As this volume shows, the military and domestic political problems soon became the major preoccupation not only of *PM*'s editorials but also of its cartoonists.

As we will see in the cartoons about the period leading up to the war, America was divided about the right strategies. A 1939 Gallup poll showed that

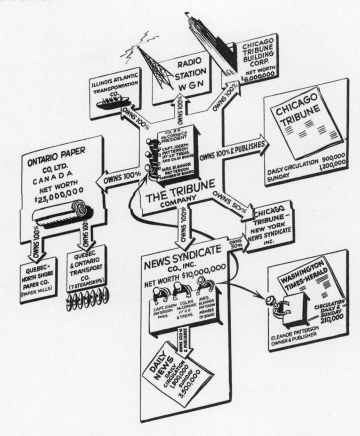

an overwhelming 84 percent of the country wanted the Allies to win (only 2 percent hoped for a German victory), but the vast majority of the country opposed going to war. Roosevelt, for all his pro-ally sentiments, did not dare suggest otherwise. In spite of this, two thirds of the country's dailies had opposed FDR in 1936; three quarters in 1940 would do so. Roosevelt saw *PM* as an important ally and the White House had many subscriptions. This access to the president and his staff, not to mention his wife, meant a great deal to Ingersoll.

Though the rest of the press was stacked against the president, there were important exceptions apart from *PM*. Walter Winchell, the *Daily News* gossip columnist, was strongly pro-FDR and his newspaper column was circulated to 9 million readers. His staccato Sunday-evening broadcast was heard by 25 million (matching Bob Hope's audience). Initially, Winchell (he would eventually move far rightward) was very close to *PM*'s politics and even wrote a special column attacking the fifth column, its ideas parallel to those expressed by *PM* and by Dr. Seuss in the early 1940s. The fifth columnists were the traitors boring from within, and both attacked the pro-Nazis in those strong terms. Hearst was unhappy about this and began to censor his writing, though Winchell was too important an asset to drop. In time, Winchell would write a column for *PM* under the pen name of Paul Revere.

In addition to the liberal columnists, Eleanor Roosevelt's "My Day" was widely circulated. Another exception to the media's right-wing output was radio. Many of the country's most famous broadcasters were strongly pro-ally, particularly those based abroad, like Edward R. Murrow, whose broadcasts from London galvanized the listening audience. The most famous broadcasters—Elmer Davis, Charles Collingwood, Howard K. Smith, and H.V. Kaltenborn—were listened to faithfully every evening by millions and wielded enormous influence on the questions of intervention and support for the allies. The White House felt, understandably, that they had total support from that medium.

As we shall see from *PM*'s cartoons, however, its overall support was far from universal.

Interventionists, Isolationists, and America Firsters

Dr. Seuss was an avowed enemy of the isolationists and he devoted many of his three cartoons a week during 1940 and 1941 to withering critiques of their spokesmen. But as Minear has pointed out in *Dr. Seuss Goes to War*, he attacked them all, regardless of their backgrounds and stances.

Those opposing America's entry into the war were certainly varied, in spite of Seuss's amalgamations. Many were still appalled by the horrors of World War I and the injustices that had resulted from it. Some, like Norman Thomas, the Socialist Party's perennial

presidential candidate, were opposed on traditional pacifist lines, which had led the Socialists to oppose World War I as well.

Others feared that American intervention would help the British maintain its empire. And after the Hitler-Stalin pact, the Communists opposed the war with many of the arguments used by those on the far right. The progressive Republican Gerard Nye of South Dakota had been responsible for major prewar congressional investigations into the profits made during the first war by the banks and the arms deal-

Yes—By All Means—Listen, and Think!

ers, the "merchants of death," as they came to be known. He would later propose ways of limiting the profits in World War II, which even Roosevelt would favor. Far from being a classic reactionary, he was to Roosevelt's left on certain key issues, favoring an end to the American embargo on arms for the Spanish Republican government, while keeping it for the Fascist insurgents. (Roosevelt, in fact, was not required by the Neutrality Act to have stopped arms to the Republic, because the act did not apply to civil wars. Toward the end of the conflict, he did allow small arms shipments to be sent through France. The major attempt at help came too late. Roosevelt finally agreed to send 150 planes, old and new, that might have been crucial, but these came just as the British persuaded the French to close the Spanish border.)

Senator Burton Wheeler had also started as a progressive Democrat but would move increasingly rightward as the war progressed. Though their 1940 presidential candidate Wendell Willkie agreed with Roosevelt on aid to Britain, the congressional Republicans were the staunchest opponents of such intervention. In 1941, Roosevelt's massive $7 billion Lend-Lease Act passed Congress with a strong majority, though 135 of the 159 House Republicans voted against the bill, as did 17 of the 27 Republican senators.

Both Hamilton Fish, the butt of many Seuss cartoons, and those at rallies of the most extreme isolationist group America First warned that Roosevelt was conspiring to bring America into the war. The isolationist *Chicago Tribune* and Hearst's New York flagship, the *Journal American*, accused Roosevelt of "deliberately trying to create an incident that would involve us in a war without constitutional Congressional declaration."[3] These conspiracy charges would resurface for many years after Pearl Harbor, which many on the right continued to believe was precisely such a conspiracy.

Seuss's major target was Colonel Charles A. Lindbergh, the heroic aviator whose solo flight across the Atlantic in 1927 had made him an American icon, and whose support Roosevelt continued to hope he could woo. But Lindbergh had accepted the idea that Germany would win, not entirely unreasonable at the beginning of the war, and that it would be folly to try to oppose it in Europe. In May 1939, he made a speech saying that Roosevelt, not Hitler, was trying to dominate the world and calling for new leadership in the United States. His wife, Anne Morrow Lindbergh, had also written a book seeing Germany as the wave of the future. *PM* editorially made Lindbergh a target of continued attacks. Ingersoll would excerpt his speeches and run a parallel column of excerpts from Germany's brilliant propaganda minister, Joseph Goebbels, showing their similarity. On August 6, 1940, Ingersoll wrote a very strong editorial, which he liked so much that he reprinted it later, in which he ended by saying he was convinced that Lindbergh was a Nazi—a conclusion Roosevelt also came to but could only confide to his close associates. Ingersoll could say it loudly, and repeatedly, in the pages of *PM*.

America First was closely linked to the most extreme anti-Semites. Father Charles E. Coughlin's broadcasts were heard by many millions, appealing to a populist base of poor Catholics. Though initially pro-Roosevelt, he moved closer to a Mussolini type of Fascism and became increasingly anti-Semitic. In time, roving mobs of his supporters would attack Jews in the streets, as did the followers of British Fascist Oswald Mosley in London. *PM* would make a point of concentrating on Coughlin and urging the government to ban his newspaper, *Social Justice*, from the mails. It succeeded in April 1941, when the paper was found to violate the just-passed Espionage Act (which must have been one of the laws least concerned with the First Amendment). Seuss published many cartoons on

Coughlin, most of which can be found in *Dr. Seuss Goes to War* but with enough left for a sampler in these pages.

Mischa Richter also linked Coughlin with Henry Ford, who managed to combine a history of vicious anti-Semitism with a violent anti-labor policy (see page 64). Ford early on printed in his newspaper the infamous *Protocols of the Elders of Zion*, a totally fraudulent document dating back to czarist Russia, which accused Jews of drinking Christian blood and the like. It was a favorite of Hitler's, who decorated and revered Ford and emulated some of his arguments. (Hitler had Ford's portrait on his wall.)

Ford paid for the *Dearborn Independent*, a paper that reached a national audience of 700,000 with arguments as odious as those in Coughlin's *Social Justice*. It was closed in 1927 after a successful libel suit. *PM* was not as aggressive in attacking Ford as Coughlin, as can be seen by the few cartoons reproduced here.

However, in September 1941, Lindbergh went too far for the American public. In a major, nationally broadcast address to an America First rally, he spoke of the groups pushing the country to war, the British and the Jewish "race." He could understand the Jews' anger at Germany and condemned their persecution there but argued that their prowar policy would be a danger for America and for them. Lest anyone miss the point, he added that the Jews should be opposing the war because "they would be the first to suffer its consequences" (something that Hitler too had warned in Europe). "The greatest danger to this country," he continued, "lies in their [the Jew's] large ownership and influence in our motion pictures, our press, our radio and our government."[4]

In spite of the prevailing anti-Semitism, this was too much. Both Lindbergh and America First were widely condemned. Even the Hearst press came out strongly against both, and America First proved very inept in answering the charges, saying it was the others who had brought race into the debate. Roosevelt would, nonetheless, later try to woo Lindbergh and persuade him to join his administration. But he failed and ended up saying to his colleagues that he was absolutely convinced that Lindbergh was a Nazi.

Seuss and others in *PM* enjoyed suggesting that Lindbergh and others were repeating the arguments of Joseph Goebbels. He certainly had a genius for coming up with arguments that made sense to those on the right in the United States and elsewhere. When, for instance, the Vichy government was established in France, the Hearst press claimed that it showed Europe was ready to cooperate with Germany in the reorganization of a united Europe, which was the Nazi claim. Later, in 1944, when Germany was clearly losing the war to Russia, Goebbels argued that it was the only defense of Western civilization against Soviet control, an argument that was repeated by some on the American right and even the collaborators, or those close to them, in France. However, it is impossible to tell how many of these arguments would have occurred anyway to Lindbergh and others. Goebbels certainly helped reinforce these ideas and perhaps did plant them, as Seuss suggests.

After Pearl Harbor, even the staunchest isolationists, like Hamilton Fish and Lindbergh, all rallied round the flag. But their arguments would resurface as the war progressed. When Hitler finally attacked Russia in 1941, many on the American right argued that the United States should not defend the communist regime, but let the two opponents fight it out. Senator Wheeler argued against helping Stalin, and a leading Republican spokesman, Robert A. Taft, went further, stating, "The victory of communism in the world would be far more dangerous to the United States than a victory of Fascism," which one can argue was a further victory for Goebbels's arguments, though again one that had strong American roots.

As the war progressed, some on the right also argued that America should concentrate on the Pacific front rather than creating the second front in Europe that Stalin was constantly demanding (though, curiously, the threat of a Stalinist-controlled Europe did not seem a credible counterargument to those making this case). Yet, as the Soviet troops pressed farther into Europe, Wheeler emerged as the champion of Polish independence. On January 17, 1945, I.F. Stone wrote a long attack on Wheeler's stand (illustrated by a Bernstein cartoon) pointing out that Wheeler had shown no such concern for the Poles when the Germans invaded and had instead argued that war could have been averted had Poland given in to all of Germany's many territorial demands. Now he argued against their "brutal conquest" by the Soviets. Wheeler referred to the alliance with Russia as "an ugly offspring born of mutual peril." Stone was in no mood to consider the horrors of Stalin's policies, such as allowing the Polish defenders of the Warsaw uprising to be annihilated while his troops waited nearby. His concern was only Wheeler's double standard.

In 1941, Stone had gotten to interview Wheeler, who then was arguing for peace negotiations with Germany, saying that we had to risk trusting Hitler, since we'd gotten along with tyrants in the past. He wanted to defend only the Western Hemisphere, north of the equator, which Stone argues would have given Hitler control over much of the world. At the time he told Stone that "some fanatics who want to get us into the war . . . will brand me a Laval or something worse," a judgment which Stone suggested would indeed become his political epitaph.

Racism: Anti-Jewish, Anti-Black, and Anti-Asian

It is hard for today's readers to grasp the degree to which the United States in the 1940s was a very racist country. *PM*'s goals included a strong stance against most of these sentiments, as part of its anti-Fascist position. But there was a major exception to its anti-racism, and, as we shall see, its pages reflected the very strong anti-Japanese sentiments that were current even before Pearl Harbor.

PM certainly opposed anti-Semitism, which was a consistent part of American life, ranging from the genteel exclusion of Jews from country clubs to mob violence on the streets of major cities, urged on by Father Coughlin and other Fascists. As we shall see below, the State Department and even to a degree Roosevelt himself shared some of the more gentlemanly versions, with disastrous results as America came to face the Holocaust.

In a series of public opinion polls taken from 1938 to 1941, over half of the American population felt that Jews were greedy and dishonest. During the war years, 56 percent thought that Jews had "too much power in the U.S., especially in finance, business and later, in government and politics." Some went even further: "from August 1940 through the war, 15–24 percent of respondents saw Jews as a menace to America . . . as much as 35–40 percent of the population would have approved an anti-Jewish campaign."[5]

PM was published in a city that housed half the nation's Jews. Many of its reporters were Jewish and a great deal of its attention, as we shall see, was devoted to prejudice in the city and to the arguments of Fascist or neo-Fascist ideologues, such as Coughlin and Ford. But, for the most part, its cartoonists did not feel able to deal with these underlying attitudes.

German persecution of the Jews was another question. When the Nazis organized the pogroms of Kristallnacht, the night of broken glass, on November 9–10, 1938, they followed with a series of draconian measures, suggesting what would follow. They imposed a fine of 4 billion marks on Germany's Jews while forbidding them access to trades, schools, universities, and even libraries. Jews were forbidden to go to concerts and theater, even to drive. All the adult Jewish men in Frankfurt were arrested and sent to concentration camps. Ninety-four percent of the Americans polled disapproved. The German ambassador in Washington, Hans-Heinrich Dieckhoff, warned that "Even the respectable patriotic circles which were thoroughly anti-Semitic began to turn away from us."[6] *PM* would find that linking American prejudices with the Nazis was an effective device, one that Seuss and the others used constantly, as did the *PM* editorials.

As we shall see, much attention was paid, especially by Seuss, to the hatemongers and to the anti-Semitic statements of people like Lindbergh. In addition to this, Seuss constantly drew cartoons attacking the bias against blacks and Jews in the war effort. There are numerous cartoons (such as on page 85) devoted to the subject. But the images are usually vague. The people involved are, for the most part, not depicted. They are labels affixed to objects denoting the war effort, such as factories or tanks. The one cartoon that depicts blacks and Jews has two identical figures, one with darker skin. Perhaps Seuss wished to avoid drawings that might have invoked stereotypes. His most striking cartoon is of the frazzled bird he often used to symbolize Uncle Sam, locked into stocks, saying "I am part Jewish."

But there are no cartoons by him or his colleagues accompanying *PM*'s lengthy effort to eliminate racist ads for employment, housing, or hotels, ads that even ran in the *New York Times*. This campaign occupied a

great deal of space and time in the papers during the 1940s. *PM* succeeded in having New York State ban these ads, though not the practice itself.

PM also pioneered in attacking unfair wages for black workers, showing that black domestic workers in New York were being paid $1.05 per hour. (In 1935, Governor Talmadge had complained to Roosevelt that WPA wages were competing unfairly with the prevailing agricultural wage scale of 40 to 50 cents a day for ten to twelve hours, giving a black farm laborer 60 to 75 dollars a year on which to live.)

Anti-black sentiment was not only widespread but also institutionalized. Segregation was assumed to be normal and could be found in all fields, including employment, housing, and education. Even the Red Cross segregated black blood among its donations, for fear that a white soldier might be accidentally contaminated. Because of the stranglehold of Southern Democrats in the Senate, legislation abolishing the poll tax, or even lynching (by then a largely symbolic bill), was blocked by the threat, and reality, of the filibuster. Roosevelt, for the most part, went along with this Southern veto, depending as he did on the electoral votes of the Southern Democrats, who were kept in power by a tiny fraction of the voters because of the very racist laws they were able to maintain. The poll tax, which Seuss and *PM* opposed continuously, completely distorted the American political scene. Not only were black voters in the South completely excluded, but so were a large number of the poorer whites. When the tax was finally abolished in Florida in the 1940s, Democrats calculated that 70 percent of white voters had also been excluded. As a result, the Southern Democrats often were elected by as few as 10 percent of their constituents. Others in Congress who actually represented the vast majority of Americans were thus stymied by a small number of racists, who, benefiting from seniority as well as the threat of the filibuster, could—and did—obstruct many of Roosevelt's policies, both foreign and domestic.

With the 1944 election, Roosevelt turned more to the big-city machine bosses in the North, whose power depended increasingly on the blacks who had migrated there during the war. Typically, Roosevelt hoped to balance both blocs. But the cracks in the

Democratic alliance were growing and would culminate in the 1948 elections, when the Southern Dixiecrats broke off and ran their own ticket. Though this did not last beyond 1948, it was the de facto basis for Nixon's Southern strategy, which gradually persuaded the South that, in spite of Lincoln's having emancipated the slaves, they were Republicans at heart. In the 2008 election, the Deep South was the one region that voted more heavily against Obama than it had against Kerry four years before.

Because of the power of the Southern Democrats in the 1930s, when Roosevelt came to power, much of the New Deal legislation failed to help the black population. Wartime production, the key to America's recovery after the collapse of the economy during Roosevelt's second term, would have continued to be segregated had A. Philip Randolph's threatened March on Washington not finally forced Roosevelt to establish the FEPC, the Fair Employment Practices Commission, in 1942. This finally abolished different pay scales and other racist practices in the nation's war industries, a policy which *PM* strongly advocated.

America would have to wait until after the war to abolish segregation in the armed forces, something that President Truman was able to do with the proverbial stroke of a pen in 1948. But the wartime segregation was not only due to the Southern Democrats. Roosevelt's secretary of war Henry Stimson defended it himself, stating that he would not use the army in wartime as a "sociological laboratory." But behind these excuses were the old familiar attitudes, Stimson

believing that "blacks lacked courage, mechanical aptitude and the capacity for leadership."[7]

In both the South and in Northern cities, racist feelings were exacerbated by blacks looking for work in war industries. A massive migration from the segregated South had led upwards of a million blacks to seek work in the North; some calculate as many as 1.6 million (another 5 million moved around the South, presumably leaving their miserable life as agricultural workers). Some 2 million blacks ended up working in war production. With the new FEPC guaranteeing equal wages, this transformed the average income for this once totally oppressed minority.

Tensions grew as the newcomers competed for jobs and homes, and racist agitators, such as Gerald L.K.

Smith in Detroit, also did their best. Riots occurred in cities as varied as Mobile, Alabama, Los Angeles (there against Chicanos as well); and most notoriously, Detroit. There, in June 1943, a two-day riot broke out with thirty-four people killed, mostly black. Federal troops restored a tense peace and Roosevelt condemned mob violence but "ducked the racial issue as he did generally during the war."[8] *PM* covered the Detroit riots extensively, amid fears that they might spread to New York. A small riot in Harlem did follow and *PM* became more militant, backing the congressional campaign of Adam Clayton Powell, a black candidate, and covering racist conditions in the New York area, segregated schools, and the like.

PM's cartoonists commented on the riots (as on page 99) when it showed the symbol of Jim Crow being decorated by Hitler. The paper covered these events extensively as well as the growing racial tensions that manifested themselves within the armed forces. (Studs Terkel's *"The Good War"* brought out, for the first time, the degree of interracial conflict within the army, which even led to black soldiers in oppressive segregated units killing their white officers.)

But the most damaging of the wartime racist feelings were those against the Japanese.

I will not repeat here the excellent analysis provided by Richard Minear, a leading historian of America and Japan, in *Dr. Seuss Goes to War*. He describes in detail the racism of Seuss, in his depiction of Japanese, both at home and abroad. Seuss, of course, was hardly the only *PM* cartoonist to show these feelings. Even Arthur Szyk, whose condemnation of Nazi oppression of the Jews was so powerful, sank to racist stereotypes when describing the Japanese leadership (as in pages 238, 246, and 247). Gross and exaggerated as his portraits of the Nazis may be, they still conveyed their features in a credible and accurate way. The Japanese, as was the case with Seuss and others, simply fit racial stereotypes.

The portrait of Japanese in America as willing tools of their overseas masters (as in *Dr. Seuss Goes to War*, page 65) helped to create the public opinion that led to Roosevelt's shameful incarceration of all 110,000 Japanese and Japanese Americans in the United States in 1942. Interestingly, the order did not apply to Hawaii, where there were simply too many Japanese Americans to put into internment camps. In spite of Hawaii's much greater proximity to the Asian war theater and in spite of the bitterness that they must have felt over the treatment of the brethren in the mainland, there were no reports of any problems during the war. (While the Supreme Court shamefully allowed this massive violation of rights, the courts were far more effective in defending the rights of Germans in the German American Bund and other pro-Nazi groups. They threw out conviction after conviction, arguing that the government had failed to completely prove intention to act subversively.)

The racist feelings about the Japanese affected more than the domestic scene. As John Dower has shown in his magisterial *War Without Mercy*, the fighting in the Pacific reached levels of hatred and brutality that were not shown in the battles in Western Europe (though Dower does not mention the horrors of the German invasion of Russia and Eastern Europe). But its effect is also shown in the glee with which *PM*'s cartoonists depicted the ravages of war in Japan, particularly the bombing raids. From Seuss's celebration of the first Doolittle raids on Tokyo on to Hiroshima, *PM*'s cartoonists faithfully echoed American public opinion. Minear describes the controversy over Seuss's attack on the Protestant cleric John Haynes Holmes for referring to the Japanese as his brothers. While Seuss defended his stance, an impressive number of *PM* readers wrote in to protest it. [9]

Perhaps the strongest example of this attitude is Melville Bernstein's cartoon on page 267, which appeared right after Hiroshima. The image is one of blank space, with a caption saying "so sorry." That phrase had been used throughout the war, usually as "so solly," to mock Japanese hypocrisy. In this case it became an indirect indictment of America's own inability to understand—and repent—the horror of the atomic attacks.

PM and the Holocaust

Considering *PM*'s progressive politics, it is surprising to note how little its cartoonists—and reporters— were initially concerned with the Holocaust. Like the rest of the mainstream American press, it ignored earlier reports sent out by the Jewish Telegraphic Agency. As early as July 1941, the New York Yiddish-language dailies reported on the murder of hundreds of Jews in Eastern Europe. No one on the *PM* staff seems to have read these newspapers, whose politics were, after all, very close to their own. By mid-March 1942, reports came from Jewish organizations that 240,000 Jews had been killed in Ukraine. In May 1942, news from Poland came that 700,000 Jews had already been gassed, a report broadcast by the BBC. But *PM*, like most of the American press, became involved only after the historic press conference by Rabbi Steven Wise in November 1942, which informed the American public of the Holocaust that was taking place, and which *PM* covered extensively.

After that, *PM* made up for lost time, by running some three hundred articles, fifty on its front page. But lacking foreign correspondents, it focused largely on the growing number of protests taking place in America and later on the question of emigration to Palestine. The full extent of the Nazi crimes did not become clear to its readers until the liberation of the camps.

Since *PM* was launched at the fall of France (June 1940), it can not be criticized for events before that

date. But it is interesting to note that Eric Godal, its very prolific German-born cartoonist, began to comment on the issue in April 1938 in a cartoon in *Ken* magazine, showing the wandering Jew. This appeared as Roosevelt announced a conference in Evian, France, to which representatives of thirty-three countries were invited to discuss the refugee problem. But the conference was a total failure, with no one in those Depression-ridden years ready to allow more Jews into their countries. The only exception was the Dominican Republic, which allowed five hundred visas for those ready to undertake agricultural work, doubtless the explanation of Steinberg's presence there in 1940. Roosevelt's own attempts to allow more Jews into the United States were systematically blocked by Congress. Even a curious attempt to subsidize emigration to Alaska was firmly opposed by that territory's legislature.

Later that year, after the state-organized pogroms of Kristallnacht on November 16 and again on November 21, the *Christian Science Monitor* ran a cartoon urging help to the refugees that Hitler was still willing to expel. (As we have seen, 94 percent of Americans disapproved of the Nazi acts, which helped the Jewish community to organize boycotts of German goods.)

The first *PM* cartoon appears to have been a curious image by Seuss on August 20, 1942. It centers on the pro-German French dictator Pierre Laval, for whom Seuss expressed an exceptional loathing. Laval is shown sharing sheet music with Hitler while Jews are hanged on trees in the background. Minear is puzzled by the fact that most Americans were ignorant of the death camps that early on. But systematic French deportation of foreign Jews had begun in May and June 1942. Seuss was either being prescient or possibly symbolic about the fate of France's Jews, 75,000 of whom would ultimately be murdered by the Germans. (The image of people hanging from trees was familiar to Americans from the photos of lynchings, which had been frequent in the period after World War I well into the 1930s, but had nearly disappeared by 1940—with two recorded in 1939—but with a surprising increase during the war.)

PM did what it could to cover the events in France, reporting on August 6, 1942, that foreign Jews were about to be deported from the German-occupied northern zone and that ten thousand more might be deported from the Vichy-controlled southern sector. On August 26, it was reported that four thousand Jewish children had been arrested by the Laval government. But that story, which might have been expected to reach a wide audience, particularly in New York, was relegated to a few lines on page 18, in spite of

PM's hatred of Laval. The placement was similar to the way in which the *New York Times* downplayed Holocaust news during all those years or stressed Nazi atrocities while barely mentioning the Jewish victims.

Arthur Szyk's many cartoons began to appear in 1943. He had been sent to the United States by the British and Polish exile governments (which, at the time, he supported) to help form anti-Nazi opinion in America. He drew for many papers and on June 1, 1943, had a cartoon in the *New York Post* protesting the recent Bermuda Conference in which Britain and America had again refused to help the refugees. *PM* ran articles on October 17 protesting that the

"Only God can make a tree
To furnish sport for you and me!"

State Department was blocking aid to European Jews. Again, on December 14, it ran a front-page story debunking the government's claims to be helping the Jews. But few cartoons accompanied these stories.

Szyk's cartoons became increasingly bitter as the situation worsened (and as he learned that his own family in Poland had been murdered). His cartoon on page 235 is dedicated to their memory. It shows Hitler and the leading Germans pleased with the death of 2 million Jews, fearing that they will soon run out. Sadly, Szyk was far too optimistic, since the Germans would find another 4 million to kill (not to mention all the others massacred in Eastern Europe). Mrs. Roosevelt was equally optimistic in her praise of the cartoonist, famously saying, "this is a personal war of Szyk against Hitler and I do not think that Mr. Szyk will lose this war." As has been mentioned above, Szyk, for much of the war, backed the Bergson group that lobbied extensively for more help.

The Bermuda Conference in the spring of 1943 had been called to deal with the refugee problem and *PM*'s coverage complained that Jews were not mentioned specifically. Clearly Roosevelt was afraid of seeming committed to helping the Jews per se, which the leaders of the American Jewish establishment accepted, fearing that the appearance of a "Jewish war" would lead to further anti-Semitism at home.

At that time, better organized protests proliferated, and an emergency conference on the Holocaust received widespread coverage. Max Lerner's *PM* editorial "What about the Jews, FDR?" was one of the strongest, charging that the State Department was averting its eyes and arguing that "You, Mr. President, must take the lead. . . . The methods are clear . . . the time is now."[10] Even the Hearst press joined in the campaign, Hearst personally ordering his thirty-four papers to run editorials supporting the conference's program.

Later in 1943, on October 3, Godal returned to the charge, attacking the State Department's lack of interest in reports of genocide. The department's notorious anti-Semitism and its successful efforts to block Jewish emigration had, however, been largely unnoticed by *PM*'s cartoonists. Because of the State Department's policies, "only 21,000 refugees were allowed to enter the United States during the three and a half years the nation was at war with Germany . . . ten percent of the number who could have been legally admitted under the immigration quotas during that period."[11]

From late 1943 through 1944, the *New York Post* ran many more cartoons than did *PM* on the issue of Palestine and the possibility of Jews finding refuge there. A *Post* cartoon attacked Roosevelt, who, having on May 30, 1944, supported the idea of free ports for refugees, then said that other countries, not the United States, should offer this help. At that time, the issue of helping Hungary's 900,000 Jews, then being deported by Eichmann to Auschwitz, also preoccupied the *Post*'s cartoonists, but not *PM*'s. However, the paper spoke very strongly on the issue of

Palestine and the rights of Jews to seek refuge there, as well as their right to fight in special Jewish brigades, a cause very dear to Szyk's heart.

Finally, Bergson's efforts resulted in the creation of a War Refugee Board to try and help the Jews and other civilian victims of the Nazi and Axis powers. Though Roosevelt objected to this effort as well, the board did have tangible results in the very last years of the war. Historians like David Wyman calculate that it may have saved as many as 200,000 lives, though the board refused to make official estimates. To be fair, when Roosevelt met with the Saudi dictator, Ibn Saud, on his way home from the Yalta Conference, he tried repeatedly to persuade him to allow all of ten thousand Jews into Palestine. Saud paid no attention to him and answered in terms so "terrible" that FDR refused to report them to his own colleagues.[12]

As the war in Europe drew to a close, Godal drew numerous cartoons, not included in this volume since they go beyond our cutoff point, on civilization's collective responsibility for the Holocaust. On July 19, 1945, he drew a cartoon of a Polish soldier carrying *Mein Kampf*, stomping on a synagogue. Presumably, this was based on early reports of Poland's anti-Jewish pogroms after the war, though *PM* does not seem to have covered those (nor did many other American papers).

In 1946, *PM* gave extensive coverage to Stone's articles about joining the refugees seeking illegal passage to Palestine, published later in his book *Underground to Palestine*. But this was an assignment that Stone took on himself, not one given him by the paper. It did help *PM*'s circulation, which rose to 150,000 to 165,000 the year it ran.

In 1945, when the camps were liberated, *PM* ran many articles and photographs of what was found. Eric Godal's most relevant cartoon, on November 27, 1944, shows a German with blood on his hands, interestingly a civilian, not someone in a Nazi uniform or bedecked with swastikas (see page 258). He faces an accusing hand, quoting a War Refugee Board report that "charges Germans tortured millions to death—Jews and Christians alike—all over Europe."

While the cartoon is correct in pointing out that millions died in addition to the Jews, the cartoon deliberately avoids the Holocaust as such. It may be that the newspaper, with its many Jewish reporters, wished to avoid an appearance of special pleading. This was, after all, the position of the far more conservative *New York Times*. But in both cases, they were appearing in a city that contained half the country's Jewish population.

While *PM* played a pioneering role in exposing and combating anti-Semitism in the city, its relative silence, in words and cartoons, on the early coverage of the Holocaust is puzzling. Paul Milkman's excellent book on *PM*, while detailed on the domestic efforts, clearly found little to report on this aspect of the foreign front. Ray Hoope's exhaustive biography of Ingersoll does not have the word *Holocaust*, or even *Jews*, in its index. It is certainly possible that this issue was of less interest to him than it was later to Max Lerner, I.F. Stone, and other *PM* writers.

Given *PM*'s commitment to the major social issues, and its strong anti-Fascist stance that led it to argue for the support of the Allies from its very inception, this gap is difficult to understand. Even without strong overseas coverage, *PM* could have covered the news that was being reported in the United States and in Britain well before November 1942. In this respect, it shared the failure of the American press as a whole.

Important Dates

Oct. 3, 1935	Italian invasion of Ethiopia
May 1, 1937	U.S. Neutrality Act
July 7, 1937	Sino-Japanese War
Oct. 1, 1938	German seizure of Sudetenland (Czechoslovakia)
Nov. 9, 1938	Kristallnacht pogrom in Germany
Sept. 1, 1939	German invasion of Poland
Sept. 17, 1939	Soviet Union occupation of east Poland
Apr. 9, 1940	German invasion of Norway and occupation of Demark
May 10, 1940	German invasion of Belgium, the Netherlands, France, and Luxembourg
June 14, 1940	German entry into Paris
July 10, 1940	Battle of Britain (to Spring 1941)
Nov. 5, 1940	Roosevelt victory over Wendell Willkie in Presidential election
June 22, 1941	German invasion of Soviet Union
Aug. 1, 1941	U.S. ban on gasoline export to Japan
Sept. 15, 1941	German siege of Leningrad (to Jan. 1943)
Sept. 30, 1941	German attack on Moscow (to December 1941)
Dec. 7, 1941	Japanese attack on Pearl Harbor, Wake, Guam, Philippines, British Malaya, Hong Kong, and Thailand
Dec. 8, 1941	U.S. declaration of war on Japan
Dec. 11, 1941	U.S. declaration of war on Germany and Italy
Jan. 20, 1942	Nazi decision on "Final Solution" at Wannsee Conference
Feb. 15, 1942	Singapore surrender to japan
Feb. 19, 1942	U.S. Executive order 9066, relocating Japanese Americans on the West Coast to internment camps
May 6, 1942	Allied surrender of Corregidor island (Philippines)

June 3–6, 1942	U.S. defeat of Japanese at Midway
Sept. 13, 1942	Battle of Stalingrad (to February 2, 1943)
Nov. 24, 1942	Rabbi S. Wise's press conference on the Holocaust
Jan. 14–24, 1943	Casablanca Conference
Feb. 2, 1943	Germans surrender at Stalingrad
May 12, 1943	Germans and Italians surrender in Tunisia
June 20, 1943	Detroit race riots
June 29, 1943	U.S. landings in New Guinea
July 10, 1943	Allies invade Sicily
Jan. 12, 1944	Allies land at Anzio, Italy
Jan. 27, 1944	Leningrad relieved
June 4, 1944	Americans enter Rome
June 6, 1944	Allies invade Normandy
July 9, 1944	Saipan falls
July 20, 1944	German generals' attempt to kill Hitler
Aug. 17, 1944	Paris rises against occupiers
Sept. 8, 1944	First German V2 rockets hit London
Oct. 20, 1944	U.S. forces land in Philippines
Feb. 13–14, 1945	British raids on Dresden
Apr. 1, 1945	U.S. forces land on Okinawa
Apr. 12, 1945	Roosevelt dies
Apr. 16, 1945	Last Russian offensive begins
Apr. 20, 1945	Hitler kills himself
May 7, 1945	Germans surrender unconditionally at Rheims
July 17, 1945	Potsdam Conference
Aug. 6, 1945	Atomic bomb dropped on Hiroshima
Aug. 9, 1945	Bomb dropped on Nagasaki
Aug. 14, 1945	Japan capitulates
Sept. 2, 1945	Japanese sign surrender in Tokyo Bay

Leading Up to the War

For much of 1941, *PM* and Dr. Seuss led a two-front war against the isolationists and in favor of American help to the British. Because Seuss spent such consistent energy on these twin causes, I have grouped his cartoons separately, even though there is some overlap in time with those in the section on the home front.

In the months before the war, American opinion gradually changed from uncertainty to support of the Allies. In March 1940, 43 percent saw a German victory as a threat to the United States; by July, 69 percent did. In May, only 35 percent favored aid to Britain at the risk of American involvement; in September, 69 percent did. But Americans were also opposed to entering the war. As late as November, 1941, on the very eve of Pearl Harbor, only 20 percent were in favor.[13]

Roosevelt was well aware of this and continued to promise that he would not lead the country into war. But he did everything that he could, both openly and surreptitiously, to help Britain. He was convinced that enough American aid might persuade Hitler that victory in the West would not be a sure thing. In March 1940, the first massive orders came from France and Britain for five thousand airframes and ten thousand engines. Hap Arnold, the head of the air force, was understandably afraid that this would greatly hinder America's own rearmament plans, but Roosevelt insisted. In September 1940, he gave Britain fifty destroyers, in exchange for British bases in the Western Hemisphere. But it was the Lend-Lease Act, passed in March 1941, that gave the cash-strapped British the aid they most needed. At first, aid was slow to materialize but eventually would amount to $11.3 billion, a great deal in 1940s dollars. But the act also forbade American ships from entering combat areas or using American naval ships for convoys. Gradually, Roosevelt moved from timidity to a quasiwar against the German submarines. These were the subjects of many of Seuss's cartoons. Roosevelt ordered the occupation of Greenland and in July 1941 sent 4,100 marines to Iceland to relieve the British, who had been there over a year (see page 40). Until then, the isolationists had agreed with FDR that the Western Hemisphere must be protected, but he was so persuasive in arguing for this move, very close to the coast of Norway, that even Wheeler was in agreement.

The German invasion of Russia on June 22, 1941, also helped to change the American political scene. Seuss's cartoon that day shows its dangers to Hitler, and the accompanying article jokes that "it's going to be a lot of fun getting out the Daily Worker tomorrow." Earlier in the year, the *Worker* had headlined a speech by Wheeler saying that 88 percent of Americans were opposed to the country's "being dragged into the war," a speech that the Nazi press had also highlighted. But Wheeler would now argue that America should let the Germans fight the Russians, while the *Worker* would continue to fight for all-out support of the war. *PM*'s and Seuss's support of the Soviet army was therefore not mere patriotism, it was also part of the domestic debate about having Russia as an ally.

Seuss's cartoon of August 26, 1941, reflects the Allies' fear about German influence in Persia and in the Middle East. The Germans were successful in recruiting many Arab leaders to their cause, but their efforts in Persia were soon blocked. Fearing that the Axis might cut off essential supply routes to Russia, Churchill and the Soviets invaded Iran and deposed the pro-Axis Shah.

That fall, Roosevelt escalated his efforts, short of war. On September 11, he ordered his navy to destroy threats to convoys, and the following month, after the Germans sank the American destroyer *Kearny*, killing eleven sailors, the House voted to arm merchant ships (see Seuss's cartoon shortly thereafter, on page 48). But the Republicans still opposed the bill, 113 to 39. Republican and isolationist opposition to the war would continue to preoccupy Seuss until Pearl Harbor.

At the same time, Seuss may have inadvertently helped the isolationists by constantly underplaying the danger posed by Japan. In cartoon after cartoon he portrays the Japanese as paper tigers (see page 116), fakers who present no real threat, as in his "Velly Scary" image of September 19, 1941. The Japanese are always portrayed in totally racist caricatures, as we have seen, but also as comically innocuous. Neither Seuss nor the others refer to the Japanese war in China or the incredible brutality they demonstrated there. It was only later that Steinberg (who had, after all, served in China) and Szyk referred to the Japanese war crimes.

Perhaps Seuss's cartoons were meant to be in indirect support of Roosevelt's increasingly bellicose stand toward Japan. Many historians now feel that while FDR was still relatively careful not to force a war with Germany, his tough stance toward Japan, leading to embargoes on key natural resources, made the Pacific war inevitable. Curiously, as we shall see, Seuss continued to underestimate Japanese strength even after Pearl Harbor.

May 12, 1941, Dr. Seuss

Portrait of a man on the horns of a dilemma.

June 19, 1941, Dr. Seuss

35

Said a bird in the midst of a Blitz,
"Up to now they've scored very few hitz,
So I'll sit on my canny
Old Star Spangled Fanny . . ."
And on it he sitz and he sitz.

The Great U. S. Sideshow

'And on this platform, the most amazing marvel of the age! He lives; he talks . . . yet the guy has no guts!'

July 11, 1941, Dr. Seuss

July 21, 1941, Dr. Seuss

40

We Clams Can't Be Too Careful

Cried a clam with an agonized shout,
"Don't be so aggressive, you lout!
That's Hitler's Atlantic;
You'll make the man frantic!
Good gracious, don't Stick your Neck Out!"

July 25, 1941, Dr. Seuss

July 28, 1941, Dr. Seuss

All Set to Answer the Bell

July 31, 1941, Dr. Seuss

September 5, 1941, Dr. Seuss

"Hey! Hide if you have to, but by thunder, stop nibbling!"

The Old Man of the Sea

A Symphony of Catcalls

September 30, 1941, Dr. Seuss

'Looks Like the Boys Are Changing Their Game Laws'

October 17, 1941, Dr. Seuss

The End of the Trail

October 22, 1941, Dr. Seuss

'Atta Boy, Sam-Bird! Keep Your Sword at Splitting Hairs!'

October 27, 1941, Dr. Seuss

'The Lord Giveth, and the Lord Taketh Away . . .'

The Home Front

PM's attitude to Roosevelt and to the 1940 elections is shown with embarrassing clarity in the cartoon of November 6, 1940, which starts this section. Roosevelt's opponent, Wendell Willkie, was a liberal Republican internationalist who would, in time, take positions considerably to FDR's left. His idealistic, internationalist tract *One World* (written with

Joseph Barnes, who later joined the *PM* staff) was an instant national bestseller and represented many of *PM*'s hopes.

But Roosevelt's opponent here is shown as a brute representing all the reactionary forces that *PM* opposed, some of which, like anti-Fascism and intolerance, were not among the president's top priorities. The picture of Roosevelt in the boxing ring perfectly symbolized *PM*'s idealization of the crippled FDR. Although care was taken never to photograph him in his wheelchair, Americans were aware of the effects of his polio. The physical Roosevelt was as imaginary as the political one. In his election year editorial, on July 15, 1940, Ingersoll explained his opposition to Willkie: "I

am most interested in Mr. Willkie's attitude towards the forces of Fascism in this country. If he does not feel as I do that the forces of Central European Fascism have already reached America and will go on affecting our life until it is stopped . . . I will be against him." Clearly, for *PM*, the political war it was waging was paramount.

Apart from disagreements on foreign policy, the Republicans were most successful in opposing Roosevelt on domestic issues. Faced with the cost of the war and the risk of inflation, Roosevelt argued from the start for higher taxes and major contributions to his war bond drives to siphon off some of the new money that was now pouring into the economy. (Americans were urged to put 10 percent of their wages into savings bonds, both to help pay for the massive war effort and to curb purchasing power.)

But since his setbacks after 1936, even the Democrats in Congress were reluctant to give him what he wanted. As soon as the war started (December 26, 1941) Taft had charged that FDR would use it as an excuse to control the economy (much as the GOP would accuse Obama in 2009 of using the economic crisis in the same way). Congress opposed Roosevelt's proposals for an excess-profits tax, even though the large firms were making record gains. Some continued to sell key minerals to the Japanese until the war, partly to raise domestic prices. Through 1941, trade with Japan and Germany grew and *PM* denounced the international cartels that linked Esso with I.G. Farben, Krupp with General Electric, etc.

PM and its cartoonists also argued for control of prices and profits. The GOP wanted only wages to be controlled and used public irritation at the new regulations and shortages to argue against any corporate controls. Roosevelt established an Office of Price Administration in April 1941, shortly before the War began, which went to overall price controls in April 1942. These worked remarkably well. (John Kenneth Galbraith, who worked there, would boast of its success in his memoirs.) Roosevelt hesitated for a long while to ration gas and rubber, and the items that were limited—sugar, meat, etc.—imposed minor inconveniences on people, not any real hardships.

Inflation was a real danger to workers in an economy that controlled wages, and in which prices, especially those in agriculture, were rising. The GOP tried to abolish the forty-hour week, worrying that overtime was helping the workers too much. So we see Seuss and *PM* using these questions as major domestic issues, attacking inflation and overconsumption, as well as a general unwillingness to agree that the war would require some sacrifices on the part of ordinary Americans. The overall growth of the economy, fed by the war spending, was stunning. The GNP in 1939, a relatively good year, was $91 billion. By 1945 it had nearly doubled to $167 billion. The economy was awash with new dollars and the desire to spend them.

Though Seuss often attacked the inefficiency of war production (see page 72), the overall picture was very different. In 1942, when Seuss was still complaining, American production of all war matériel was already equal to that of the three Axis powers, Germany, Italy, and Japan. By 1944, it was double their production.

On the whole, *PM* backed labor, even when it went on strikes that were very unpopular with the public, even thought to be unpatriotic (though the total man-hours lost during the war were under one tenth of one percent, a better record even than Britain's). The exception was John L. Lewis, the head of the United Mine Workers, whom *PM* attacked in several cartoons (see pages 53, 97, and 99) and many articles. Lewis was critical of Roosevelt and did not share *PM*'s New Deal views. His isolationism and backing of Willkie in 1940 earned him the paper's hatred. When he rejected arbitration, *PM* sounded like many other papers in saying he was endangering the war effort. (Compulsory arbitration was finally legislated in January 1942 with the creation of a National War Labor Board.)

PM's patriotic fervor went beyond denunciations of big business. It found numerous cases of inefficiency and underused resources which it pointed out to the government. It also pushed attacks on spies and fifth columnists and generally did all it could to mobilize public opinion for the war effort. The cartoon of an overly relaxed Uncle Sam, on February 12, 1942, invokes not only Pearl Harbor but also the fire on the *Normandie*. The French liner had been docked in New York when it accidentally burst into flame. Sabotage was suspected, though finally this was disproved.

Henry Ford was the worst of the employers in his labor policies and simply refused to accept the Wagner Act's reforms. *PM* strongly attacked him, asking for criminal indictments, likening his propaganda to Goebbels. Since the rest of the press was continuing its prewar bias against labor, reporters on other papers would come to *PM* with anti-Ford material they couldn't run themselves. *PM*'s cartoon of April 6, 1941, is a reference not just to Ford's goon squads but a joke about Seuss's famous advertising campaign, "Quick, Henry, the Flit," an image that Seuss himself recycled in his cartoons of Hitler.

PM however defended union leaders that were anathema to the rest of the press, when it felt their demands were just: Mike Quill, who ordered transit strikes in New York, and Harry Bridges, the Communist teamster leader whom Roosevelt wanted to deport to Australia. Seuss's cartoon (June 2, 1942) appeared with a *PM* editorial attacking Attorney General Biddle but, as always, would never mention Roosevelt, whose backing Biddle needed. Throughout, *PM* refused to attack the president for policies he clearly had had to approve. In all of *PM*, there is not one cartoon even vaguely critical of him.

In 1942, after Hitler's invasion of Russia, the Communist Party became strongly anti-strike and even attacked A. Philip Randolph's battle for anti-discrimination legislation. *PM* was strongly opposed to the Communist Party line but also attacked the AFL, the more conservative of the union groups, for its racism and its silence during the 1944 elections.

Curiously, *PM* did not make use of the support tendered by the unions. David Dubinsky, head of the International Ladies Garment Workers Union (ILGWU), offered to buy fifty thousand subscriptions for his union, but Ingersoll puritanically refused what would have been a major addition to his 150,000 readers.

Another of *PM*'s favorite targets was Martin Dies, whose Un-American Activities Committee was a precursor and model for Joe McCarthy's later efforts. Dies was theoretically looking for communists, which Seuss frequently mocked (June 28, 1942), as did others. When the Soviets dissolved the Comintern, its international grouping of parties throughout the world, *PM* rather naively assumed this meant the end of Soviet influence (May 24, 1943). The Communist Party USA renamed itself the Communist Political Association, but, as we now know, this had no effect on Soviet espionage, which for the most part sought to avoid using party members in any case.

Presumably this had little effect on Dies, who was not that interested in any real Soviet threat any more than McCarthy would be. As Walter Winchell argued in a radio broadcast reported in a *PM* article by James Wechsler (March 26. 1944), Dies specialized in smearing hundreds of loyal government officials, attacks about which even Attorney General Biddle complained to Congress. Dies never attacked Father Coughlin and even appeared on a public platform with one of his representatives. Wechsler, by then strongly anti-Communist himself, also cited Winchell's charge that Dies attacked "many well-known Progressive Americans who were militantly anti-Communist and who had been attacked . . . in the *Daily Worker.*"

The Third Round

"We want a knockout!"

July 22, 1940, Matt Greene

August 25, 1940, Daniel Fitzpatrick

You Too!

Billions for Defense, But Not Less Than 10 Per Cent

Cartoon by Matt

December 31, 1940,
Mischa Richter

' "I don't know them, officer, they're hitch hikers"

February 11, 1941,
Mischa Richter

Here comes an Englishman; up go the prices.'

Quick, Henry, the "tear gas"

April 6, 1941, Leo Hershfield

April 13, 1941, Leo Hershfield

The Greatest Quisling of Them All

CAGES COST MONEY! **Buy More U. S. Savings Bonds and Stamps!**

January 19, 1942, Dr. Seuss

'Champ, Ain't It About Time We Tied on the Other Glove?'

Dr. Seuss

Copyright, 1942, Marshall Field
The Newspaper PM.

That Man is Back Again.

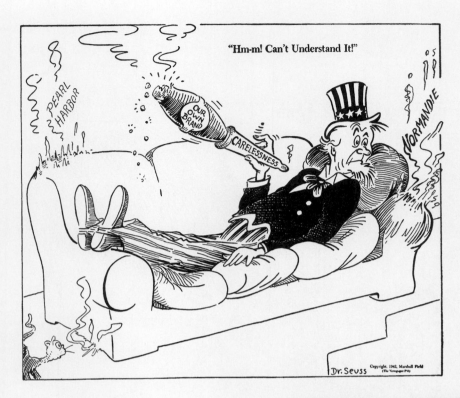

February 12, 1942, Dr. Seuss

February 20, 1942, Dr. Seuss

70

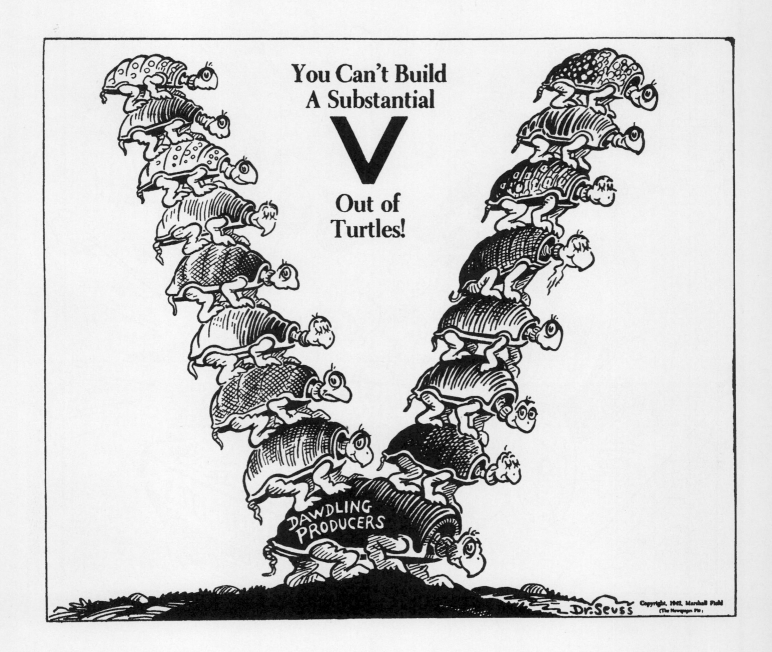

"Hold her, Newt! Get her down on the road!"

Don't Kid Yourself. If He Shoots The Works You're Sunk!

April 19, 1942, Dr. Seuss

June 2, 1942, Dr. Seuss

The OLD GRUDGE of 42d Street

Sauerkraut Symphony

A GRUDGE, blowing hard as he's able
Sits high on his own Tower of Babel,
And millions he treats
To the same brassy bleats
That Hitler oft feeds us by cable.

June 5, 1942, Dr. Seuss

Stretching for Every Autograph in Town!

June 17, 1942, Dr. Seuss

July 10, 1942, Dr. Seuss

July 18, 1942, Dr. Seuss

What Are You Chasing Most, Pal...Butterflies or Skunks?

The Guy Who Makes a Mock of Democracy

"I pledge allegiance
To the Flag of the United States
And to the Republic for which it
    stands.
One Nation indivisible,
With Liberty and Justice for
    all . . .
(Except the boys and girls
I keep down in the cellar)."

Man Power That <u>Could</u> Be Winning the War . . .

(Washington papers please copy)

Pledge of Allegiance

We give our heads
And our hearts·
To God and our Country.
One Country,
One Language,
Two Flags.

Beware the Vendor of Breakable Toys!

October 14, 1942, Dr. Seuss

October 16, 1942, Dr. Seuss

"This is our American uncle. He has been so helpful to us!"

By Steinberg

Don't Lean on It Too Hard, Pal!

December 3, 1942, Dr. Seuss

December 8, 1942, Dr. Seuss

Helium-Filled Easy Chair

December 9, 1942, Dr. Seuss

December 10, 1942, Dr. Seuss

"If peace ever breaks out, we might be caught short with too-little-and-too-late!"

December 24, 1942, Dr. Seuss

"Jeepers! Just what we asked Santa Claus not for!"

But the Piper Must Pay

January 4, 1943, Dr. Seuss

"What? You still smell something?"

May 2, 1943, Al Hirschfeld

General Lewis Starts His Offensive

**Heck,
Nobody There**

*May 24, 1943,
Melville Bernstein*

The U.S. Senate is equipped with all known devices, ancient and modern, for mutilating treaties.

June 22, 1943, Eric Godal

For Aid and Comfort to the Enemy

June 23, 1943, Eric Godal

'Nice of You to Give Me a Hand, Pal!'

"Refer to Committee 3, Investigation Subcommittee 6, Section 8B, for consideration."

November 19, 1943, Eric Godal

Herr Goebbels, you are a piker! Listen to this!

January 5, 1944, Eric Godal

"We protest! Our fourth freedom is threatened!"

February 1, 1944,
Eric Godal

Their Master's Voice

February 28, 1944,
Eric Godal

"This will stem the flood."

December 6, 1944, Eric Godal

December 28, 1944,
Eric Godal

The War Begins

PM's cartoonists were consistently optimistic in describing the European war, once it began. The newspaper's policy toward Hitler during the early years was one of mockery, paying little attention to his stunning victories. The two cartoons of September 19 and September 25, 1940, are good examples. The British air raid on Berlin of August 25, their

subject, did indeed have strong psychological effect. The Germans had not thought the British capable of reaching Berlin. But the physical damage was slight, hardly what was suggested in Groth's cartoon. It was the German retaliations on London that were truly effective, with over a thousand killed in the raids of September 7, 1940.

Nor were the German troops likely to complain of hunger, as suggested by Richter, on November 13, 1940, especially since Germany had begun its very effective and systematic plunder of Europe's food and other resources, as the cartoon of August 15, 1940 suggests (there was clearly no internal cohesion to the ideas presented in *PM*'s cartoons). Steinberg's many

jokes about Germany living on ersatz products are closer to the point. The Nazis had early on produced artificial, ersatz, substitutes for goods it could no longer import from abroad. Coffee, for instance, would be made from ground acorns, a tasteless brew that soon became standard throughout occupied Europe. But on the whole, the German population lived far better than *PM*'s cartoonists hoped.

The Seuss cartoon of June 30, 1941, refers to a real problem Japan faced since it had not only allied itself with Germany but also had signed a nonaggression pact with the Russians. In spite of Hitler's urgings, Japan decided it had enough to do conquering Southeast Asia and held to its Russian pact until the very end.

Seuss, Steinberg, and the others at *PM* were right to mock Hitler's mad hopes to conquer Russia and North Africa at the same time, but they totally underestimated the success of the German troops until their failure in late 1942 to defeat the Russians at Stalingrad. Their successes were so massive that it looked as if they might well win the war before the Americans could intervene. In addition to their total conquest of Western Europe, the Germans were winning in North Africa, where Rommel's invasion of Libya brought the Germans within reach of Egypt and the Suez Canal. The West was in no position to open the second front that the Russians desperately needed. At the same time, German submarines came close to winning the battle of the Atlantic, sinking 8 million tons of Allied and neutral shipping, bringing desperately needed supplies to Britain and to Russia. There, a quarter of American ships trying the Arctic route were sunk

In Asia, the situation was equally alarming. After their successful attack on the American fleet in Pearl Harbor, the Japanese swiftly invaded Southeast Asia, occupying Malaya, Burma, and the British stronghold of Singapore in April 1942. MacArthur had to flee the Philippines, and the Japanese were able to move on to Indonesia and even threaten Australia.

These overwhelming victories would not have been apparent to Seuss's readers, who were shown only the few American triumphs: Doolittle's surprising air raid on Tokyo, on April 18, 1942, and the major American naval victory at Midway, which stopped what might have been a Japanese invasion of Hawaii.

Throughout this disastrous time, *PM*'s cartoonists were relentlessly upbeat. On March 18, 1942, Seuss refers to Hitler's wooing of neutral Ireland. Churchill had tried to persuade the Irish to join the British cause but had failed to do so, and anti-British, and therefore pro-German, sentiment remained an important factor throughout the war. One of the few bits of good news celebrated by Seuss (May 6, 1942) was the successful defense of Madagascar from a threatened Japanese invasion. The British had seized the island colony, itself larger than its colonial master, France, in 1942, when it looked as if the Vichy government might allow the Japanese to control it, as they had done in Indochina.

Today's readers may be puzzled by the Seuss cartoon of May 14, 1942 which celebrates the United Nation's newfound vigor. The United Nations was the name the Allies chose for themselves, using it after the war for the newly created international organization we now know by that name.

Seuss and Steinberg continued their optimistic view of the war until the tide actually began to turn, when the possibility of German defeat in North Africa and Russia began to materialize.

107

July 25, 1940,
John Groth

The Artist Prepares His Masterpiece

August 15, 1940,
William Sanderson

Cartoon by William Sanderson

Adolf: Raid Berlin? How dare they!

September 25, 1940,
John Groth

"German workers, we have now achieved complete air supremacy"

November 13, 1940,
Mischa Richter

"I'm Hungry!"

By Mischa Richter

November 26, 1940,
John Groth

"Goebbels, did you see? . . . London has been completely wiped out!"
"I know, I wrote it myself."

January 9, 1941,
Mischa Richter

"And when you're through with him, you're tackling America!"

By Mischa Richter

112

"Joe Kennedy says the people of Europe are asking what they're fighting for."

August 15, 1941, Dr. Seuss

June 30, 1941, Dr. Seuss

"Training ... There's some talk he may have to spend the winter up in Russia!"

"Pssst ... Adolf!
How am I doin'?"

August 26, 1941, Dr. Seuss

August 22, 1941, Dr. Seuss

Now where's that bug
that was snug
in the Persian rug?

What's the cheery word from Russia?

September 7, 1941, Dr. Seuss

A Costume He Found in the Kaiser's Attic . . .

September 17, 1941, Dr. Seuss

Velly Scary Jap-in-the-Box . . . Wasn't It?

October 13, 1941, Dr. Seuss

October 20, 1941, Dr. Seuss

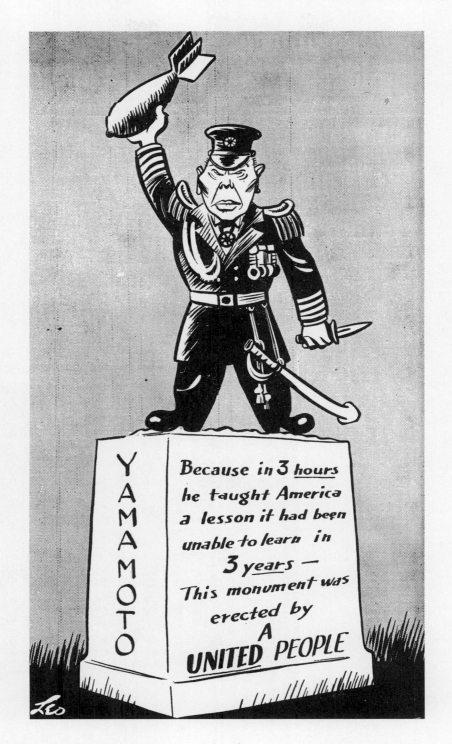

'Scram! We're busy listening to Sumner Welles!'

January 15, 1942, Dr. Seuss

The Wonders of Russian Science

January 16, 1942, Dr. Seuss

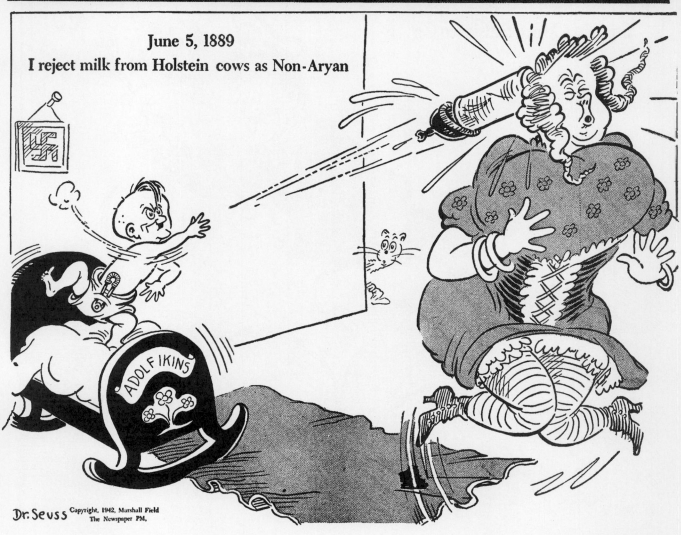

Mein Early Kampf   by Adolf Hitler

June 20, 1889

I cut my first tooth
on a Bust of Bismarck

BISMARCK

ADOLFIKINS

Dr. Seuss   Copyright, 1942, Marshall Field
            (The Newspaper PM)

Latest Modern Home Convenience
Hot and Cold Running Subs

January 22, 1942, Dr. Seuss

January 26, 1942, Dr. Seuss

The Stench
of the Scented Isles

The Tail of the Boxing Kangaroo

January 27, 1942, Dr. Seuss

January 28, 1942, Dr. Seuss

"He is a perfect Aryan ever since he bit the leg of Dr. Goebbels."

Cartoon by Steinberg

Before and After Treatments:
1939–194-?

Cartoon by Steinberg

"Private Mitsubiki, don't you know our code of honor forbids cutting a woman's throat with your cap on?"

Cartoon by Steinberg

German: First Class

Are We Mice or Are We Men?

March 29, 1942,
Carl Rose

April 5, 1942,
Carl Rose

"Plenty soon magic globe will show honorable future." *Cartoon by Steinberg*

April 27, 1942, Saul Steinberg

Junior is such an imaginative liar; when he is grown up he certainly will become an important member of the staff of Domei.

At Last, a New Weapon . . . Our Counteroctopus

May 6, 1942, Dr. Seuss

When the Punching Bag Socks the Champ—That's NEWS

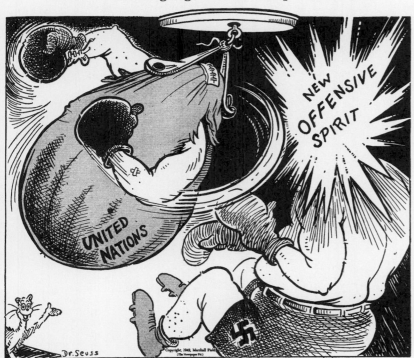

May 14, 1942, Dr. Seuss

143

May 10, 1942, Carl Rose

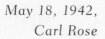

Designed Exclusively for Going UP

May 19, 1942, Dr. Seuss

"I might drive here. I might drive there. Or I MIGHT just drive around the corner for an aspirin!"

May 21, 1942, Dr. Seuss

May 29, 1942, Dr. Seuss

June 10, 1942, Dr. Seuss

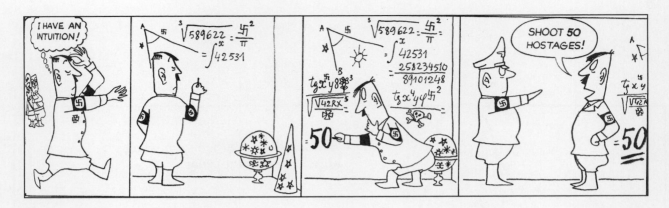

May 24, 1942, Saul Steinberg

May 31, 1942, Saul Steinberg

June 21, 1942, Saul Steinberg

July 5, 1942, Saul Steinberg

July 19, 1942, Saul Steinberg

Neutrality Mixture . . . Guaranteed to Bite the Tongue!

Goebbels: *None of them will return a Communist from the East.*

In the Bottom of the Hour Glass

July 30, 1942, Dr. Seuss

The Tiller of the Soil

August 4, 1942, Dr. Seuss

August 29, 1942, Dr. Seuss

September 29, 1942,
Dr. Seuss

September 3, 1942, Saul Steinberg

September 6, 1942, Saul Steinberg

October 4, 1942, Saul Steinberg

'There's Many a Slip . . .'

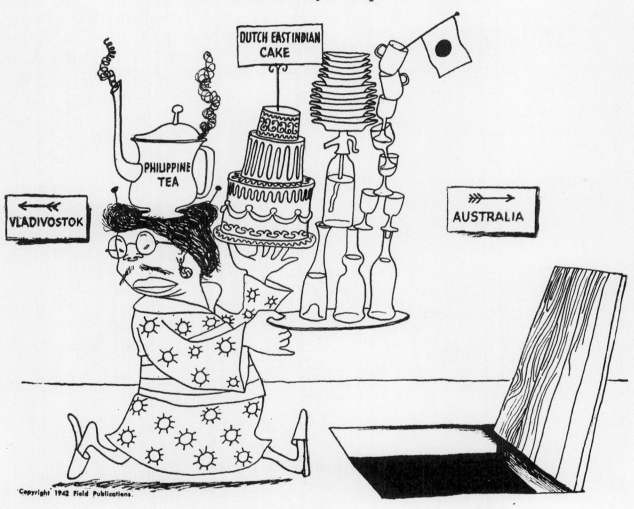

Hitler's Program for 1942

Cartoon By Steinberg

156

July 26, 1942, Saul Steinberg

August 2, 1942, Saul Steinberg

August 9, 1942, Saul Steinberg

August 16, 1942, Saul Steinberg

August 23, 1942, Saul Steinberg

August 30, 1942, Saul Steinberg

September 13, 1942, Saul Steinberg

September 16, 1942, Saul Steinberg

November 4, 1942, Saul Steinberg

It's quite inexpensive and he doesn't say less than our other propaganda agents.

The Master Race

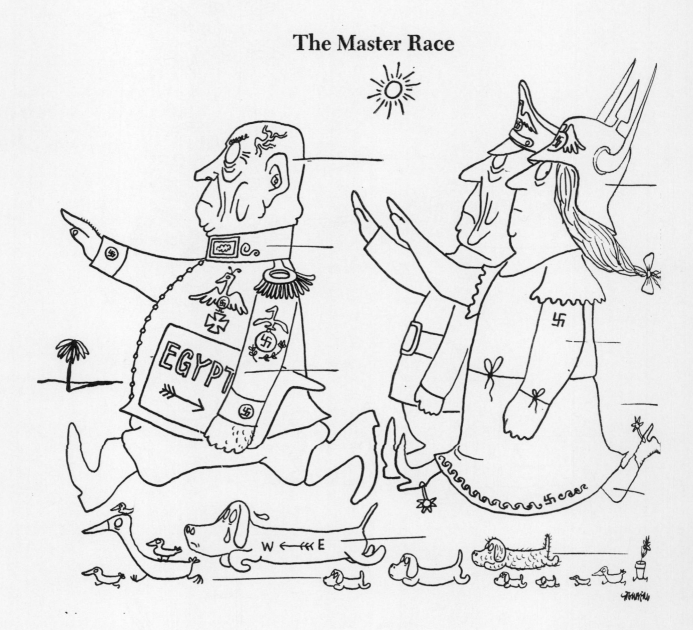

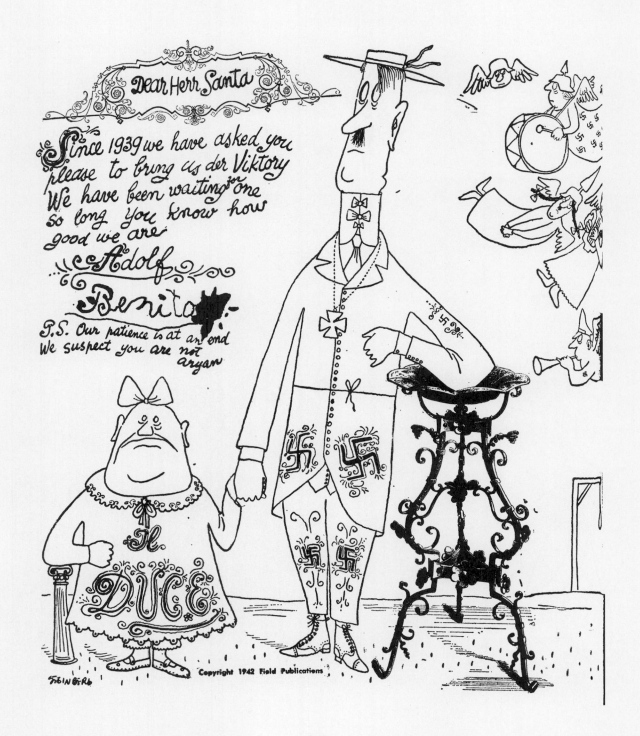

Tin Can for the Tail of the Soaring Dachshund

INSIDE GERMANY by Godal

January 10, 1943, Eric Godal

"It doesn't matter that you said nothing—I saw you *think* something!"

February 28, 1943, Eric Godal

INSIDE GERMANY by Godal

"Of course, one quick glance and you can tell the difference between a Nordic and a non-Nordic skull!"

February 7, 1943,
Eric Godal

The last meeting with his board of intuitions.

February 16, 1943,
Eric Godal

Hitler consults his intuitions on threatened Allied invasion.

Hitler's Allies

Laval, Darlan, Vichy, and the French Collaborationists

Seuss was an early and consistent critic of Vichy France and its collaborationist leaders. *Dr. Seuss Goes to War* is filled with images showing his disgust at those who betrayed France and sided with the Germans. (Marshall Pétain's prime minister, Pierre Laval, would

openly proclaim his hopes for an ultimate Nazi victory.) In these pages, we see Seuss's constant attacks on Laval, his collaboration with Hitler, his agreement to send French workers to Germany (far from the worst of his crimes) and his collaboration with the Japanese in his attempt to maintain French control over Indochina. (It's worth noting that in practically every French colony, which were all free of German troops, the local colonial governments followed Vichy with excessive zeal.)

Seuss's cartoons are also prescient in attacking Admiral Darlan, Pétain's one-time premier (with whom Roosevelt would briefly cooperate). Szyk also drew a particularly cruel portrait of Darlan and Pétain (July

13, 1941), the latter always portrayed by Seuss as a doddering, pathetic figure.

In this respect *PM* was an exception to the general coverage. As we have seen, the Hearst press actually welcomed the Vichy government as proof of Germany's new cooperative rule in Europe. The *New York Times* was also far closer to the government's line, which was guardedly pro-Vichy and hoped to persuade the Pétain government to cooperate with America. Roosevelt's ambassador, Admiral Leahy, very much encouraged these unrealistic hopes, since Pétain was entirely under German control. This also supported Roosevelt's nearly irrational dislike for General de Gaulle and the Free French opposition that he led from London.

PM was concerned early on (December 17, 1941) with the future of the French fleet. According to the armistice agreement, this important force was to be kept in mothballs for the duration of the war, much to de Gaulle's anger, who felt that it, and France's colonies, could have been essential cards in his battle against Hitler. When the United States invaded North Africa, the Germans reacted by saying the armistice terms no longer applied and took over the southern, Vichy, zone of France. In spite of Churchill's often expressed hopes that the French navy might defect, the French admiralty responded by successfully scuttling the fleet that had been anchored at Toulon, hence Seuss's cartoon of November 30, 1942. Sixty-one ships sank, totalling 225,000 tons, including three battleships, ten cruisers, twenty-eight destroyers, and fourteen submarines. De Gaulle lamented this "barren sacrifice."

Seuss's early cartoons in 1940 had attacked Admiral Darlan in Africa, where he did everything he could to collaborate with the Germans and act against both the British and the Gaullists, who were trying to bring some of France's African colonies into the Free French camp. Darlan saw himself as Hitler's ally in these endeavors.

In spite of this, Roosevelt was willing to work with Darlan when American troops landed in North Africa in 1942. Eager to limit American deaths in this prelude to the liberation of Europe, Roosevelt sent Robert Murphy, a conservative State Department official, ahead of the invasion to establish links with the local Vichy rulers of North Africa. He hoped to get their agreement not to fight the American troops when they arrived. Like Leahy, Murphy found himself at home with the local reactionaries and argued for possible Vichy collaboration. He expressed high regard for Darlan, in spite of Darlan's clear record of wanting to establish military cooperation with the Germans and his defense of Vichy's dictatorial and anti-Semitic policies.

Roosevelt also tried to appeal to Pétain, who he thought might be able to act independently of his German masters. He drafted a letter to "My dear old friend," whose fulsomeness outraged Churchill. He asked Roosevelt to "tone it down," which included replacing his ludicrous salutation. Of course, Pétain was unable, and probably unwilling, to do anything to help the American forces.

Darlan found himself accidentally in North Africa on the eve of the invasion and offered to stop French military resistance if Roosevelt would allow him to continue to run the local Vichy government. Though Roosevelt privately referred to Darlan as a skunk, he agreed, hoping to reduce American casualties as much as possible. In this, he succeeded but at the price of keeping a Fascist government in place. Darlan maintained Vichy's anti-Semitic laws, which had deprived North Africa's Jews of their long-standing citizenship and kept the prisons filled with the Gaullists, Spanish loyalists, refugees, and others who had opposed Vichy and Hitler. He even imprisoned, briefly, those who had worked with the Americans in planning their invasion. A.J. Liebling wrote scathing articles in the *New Yorker* about America's policy, and *PM* joined in a chorus of denunciation. What was the point of liberating countries if their Fascist governments were kept in place? This question would surface again as America invaded Italy and followed similar policies (see below). An additional cause for worry was Murphy's naming of another vicious Vichyite, Marcel Peyrouton, as governor of Algiers. A former Pétain minister of the interior, he was among the worst of that crew, having personally shaped Vichy's initial anti-Semitic laws. Willkie, Walter Lippmann, and many others objected strongly. *PM*'s views were shared by far more conservative spokesmen.

What none of these knew was that Roosevelt took it upon himself to negotiate privately with the Vichy governor of Morocco, Auguste Nogues, and then with General Giraud. FDR, who spoke fluent French, suggested to both that quotas for Jews in the professions be based on a quota of their proportion to the population (300,000 of more than 13 million), which would not have reopened many of the jobs that Vichy had closed. Little known as well is that he argued that "his plan would eliminate the understandable complaints which Germans bore towards the Jews, namely that while they represented a small part of the population, over 50% of the lawyers, doctors, school teachers, college professors, etc. in Germany were Jews."[14] This astonishing claim showed the degree to which FDR had accepted Nazi propaganda about the German Jews. As Freidel points out, while Jews were between 1 and 2 percent of the German population before the war, they comprised no more than 2.3 percent of the professions. At most, 16.3 percent of the lawyers had

been Jewish. While historians have agreed that Roosevelt did not do what he could have to help or later save the Jews, this is the first evidence I have seen that he himself had internalized some of the Nazi arguments about the power of Germany's Jews. But Roosevelt was no stranger to the question of quotas. Freidel, whose biography of FDR is overwhelmingly favorable, nonetheless points to his time as a member of the Harvard Board of Overseers, its governing body. In 1927, deciding against quotas, the university agreed simply to accept the brightest applicants. To its shock, 42 percent of those accepted were Jews. Harvard, with Roosevelt's approval, finally decided on a 15 percent quota for Jews (more generous than in other Ivy League schools). FDR always defended that decision and clearly he thought it an appropriate answer to Vichy's dilemma.

Roosevelt was soon freed of the Darlan problem when a young French monarchist shot Darlan dead. The monarchist, in turn, was executed immediately by the Vichy government, though it appeared that he had been given guarantees of his safety, by whom is not known.

But this experience did not stop Roosevelt's hesitation to recognize de Gaulle, who many felt should by rights have been allowed to take over the government of a free French territory. Roosevelt continued to see other possible French leaders, such as General Giraud, whom he imposed on de Gaulle as a possible partner. All these moves were attacked by *PM* and its cartoonists, who felt, as did Churchill, that de Gaulle was the clear and obvious leader of a freed France.

Roosevelt's opposition lasted into the liberation of

France when he planned to rule the country with an American military government. He even personally ordered that the AMG's printed French currency omit the words *République Française*. Only after the libera-

tion of France, faced with de Gaulle's overwhelming popularity and his effective assumption of power, did he abandon these policies, belatedly recognizing the new French government on October 23, 1944.

Hitler's Other Friends

PM was as constant a critic of Hitler's allies as it was of the French collaborationists. John Groth's cartoon from July 17, 1940, shows the Duke of Windsor and his American wife being sent off to Bermuda in 1940 for the duration of the war, to serve as its governor, safely away from Britain's shores. Windsor had been part of the sizeable pro-German circle in England's upper classes, expressing opinions that went strongly against Churchill's policies. It was feared, not unreasonably, that if the Germans succeeded in invading Britain, which seemed very possible, that they would use Windsor as the head of a pro-Nazi government, possibly with Oswald Mosley as his prime minister—the kind of quisling government that the Germans had established first in Norway, then in France and other countries. Windsor would stay in Bermuda, out of harm's way, until the end of the war.

Hitler's actual co-belligerents received ample attention in *PM*'s pages. Mussolini, above all, was treated with constant ridicule as a hopeless buffoon who was a complete failure militarily. In this respect, Seuss et al. were being somewhat indulgent. In his invasion of Ethiopia in 1935—admittedly before *PM* existed—

Mussolini had shown that he could be as brutal as Hitler. Not only did his troops, including his son, gleefully bomb defenseless villages and boast of it, they systematically murdered the small, educated elite, a policy that Hitler would later follow in Poland.

But it is true that Mussolini's first moves during World War II were not as successful. His attempts to conquer Greece and Albania floundered and Hitler was forced to send troops to take over his campaigns. Likewise, in North Africa, the Italian army did not distinguish itself and would, in time, surrender to the Allies in the hundreds of thousands. When America invaded Italy in 1942, *PM* watched warily as Roosevelt, as he had done in North Africa, agreed to collaborate with the government of King Emanuel after a Fascist coup d'etat displaced Mussolini. The Fascist leadership, unhappy with the Hitlerian alliance, named one of their own, Marshal Badoglio, to take over and negotiate surrender with the Americans. These negotiations took too long, since the Americans did not want to appear to give up their demands for unconditional surrender. Once the Americans landed on Italian soil, they announced the surrender and the Germans took over the capital. Badoglio's government fled and the civil war started that would last until the end of the war. Roosevelt was unhappy with this solution, which he had assumed would only be temporary, but he acted under pressure from Churchill, who was eager to keep the right in place in the Mediterranean, which he considered his zone of influence. Both in Italy, and later in Greece, Roosevelt feared a communist takeover and preferred to ally himself with the old reactionary monarchies, even encouraging a civil war in Greece in which he helped the right attack the former communist resistance forces. This led to *PM*'s cartoons of September 10, 1942, and February 6, 1944. The left in America understandably feared that the Darlan precedent would be followed as Europe was liberated. Joe Barnes, Wendell Willkie's co-author, who would go on to the *PM* staff, was censured for his OSS broadcasts to the Italian public saying that the American invasion would bring democratic rule.

Among the neutrals, Franco was the chief target of *PM*'s venom. Feelings on the American left were still strong about the Spanish Civil War, as was guilt about our inability to help the loyalist government. *PM* ran countless articles about Franco's pro-German stance and his active help to Hitler during the war. An early article by I.F. Stone exposed the fact that oil exports to Spain were being transshipped to Germany, which actually stopped the shipments.

Though Franco's sympathies, and debts, were clearly to Hitler, he played his cards carefully, especially as the war progressed and the tide turned. He refused Hitler's bid to have his troops cross Spain in order to bolster German defenses in North Africa and he kept a tight grip on Gibraltar. However, Franco continued to ship vital war matériel until stopped by an Allied boycott of the oil on which his economy depended. He also assisted the Nazis in Latin America, particularly in Argentina, where the government was Fascist and pro-Nazi. (Argentina in particular kept out all Jewish refugees, in spite of having a large Jewish community.) Franco also sent thousands of Spanish soldiers, as volunteers, to a likely death, fighting alongside the Germans in Russia as the Blue Division, named after the dark blue shirts of his Falangist movement. Only eighteen thousand men had initially been deployed, but replacements were sent for the fallen, so the final number was far greater. One hundred thousand Spanish workers were also sent.

As was the case in Vichy France, Roosevelt's ambassador to Madrid Carlton Hayes, was friendly to the government. A dense and ill-informed Columbia history professor, he had been enthusiastically pro-Franco during the Civil War and was soon charmed by him. But Franco was so consistently pro-German, expecting Hitler somehow to prevail until the very end, that even Hayes had to warn Washington. *PM* consistently attacked Hayes, and the press's pressure against Franco was felt in Madrid. But in spite of Roosevelt's and Hull's opposition to Franco, the State Department was responsible for petty harassment of the loyalist exiles. On November 14, 1943, *PM* ran a long article showing that the State Department was refusing a transit visa for a former Loyalist minister and his family, who simply wanted to cross the United

States in order to join the twenty thousand other loyalist exiles in Mexico.

There were a great many anti-Franco cartoons in *PM*, far too many to include in their entirety. Richter has two, early on, in February 1941. The February 28, 1941, cartoon refers to the battle of Santander, a major Fascist victory, won with Italian help. It refers sardonically to the embargo that was supposed to limit the fighting in the Civil War. The cartoons on March 8, 1944, and March 20, 1944, are among the many attacking Ambassador Hayes and the State Department's pro-Franco bias. *PM* closely followed Franco's covert aid to Hitler. The cartoon on May 18, 1944, showed Franco's closing of his consulate in Tangier, which had been used as a base for German espionage, one of several moves that Franco conceded under the pressure of the Allied oil embargo. *PM* suggested that the move was merely a cosmetic one. (The oil embargo is referred to in a cartoon of November 19, 1944.)

In 1944, *PM* also objected to America's participation at Franco's World Fair in Barcelona. More important, it hoped, as did many on the left in Europe as well as America, that the end of the war would be the end of Franco. *PM* editorialized urging help to the Republicans who hoped to reenter Spain and overthrow the Fascists. Many optimistic cartoons appeared showing the Spanish people finally rising up and ridding themselves of their noxious dictator. Attempts were made in the fall of 1944, when several hundred armed Republicans came in from the south of France, but lacking any outside governmental help, and with the opposition of the Spanish Communist Party—and

therefore of Moscow—these were doomed and soon crushed by Franco. He would stay in power another thirty years.

PM also spent a lot of time on the Argentine dictators. Right after Pearl Harbor, Secretary of State Sumner Wells called a conference in Rio to urge joint hemispheric action against the Germans (see Seuss's cartoon on page 126). America was worried about German links with Latin America, some fostered by Franco, and the military feared a possible German invasion. Those fears were exaggerated, but Nazi sympathies were strong in Argentina and Chile, both of which had a strong German emigration, as was the case in North America. Neither of these two countries agreed to break off relations after the Rio conference, while the others did. (See Seuss's cartoon on page 127. As always, Seuss followed events closely and punctually.)

In Argentina, the government was overtly sympathetic to the Nazis and their agents. In June 1943, a group of military officers took power and a new president, Edelmiro Farrell, took office in February 1944. The U.S. government tried to persuade the other Latin American governments to refuse recognition and briefly froze the Argentinean gold it was holding. Farrell's government suppressed free speech, the press, and the democratic opposition. Clearly, this was a major target for *PM* and its cartoonists. For once, it was in agreement with the State Department, which did all it could against Farrell, but the other Latin governments feared Washington's intervention more than it disliked Argentina's Nazi links. Colonel Juan Perón attacked the

U.S. policy and ran for the presidency, which he won in 1945. Even though Argentina would eventually declare war on Germany and Japan, Perón's fascistic government would stay in power for years to come. It created, through a well-organized network with Vatican help, a haven for a huge number of Nazi escapees.

PM did not hesitate to attack other neutral states that were helping the Germans. One cartoon on May 5, 1944, attacks Sweden's deliveries of iron ore to Germany, one of many shipments of crucial war matériel, such as ball bearings. I found no such cartoons when Sweden allowed German troops to cross their country by rail in order to invade their Scandinavian neighbor, Norway, an act which rankled for many years after the war.

July 17, 1940, John Groth

"Hate to see you go old man"

August 13, 1940, Daniel Fitzpatrick

Thank God for the German Army, Monsieur

"Something wrong with the big act, Adolf?"

December 3, 1940, Daniel Fitzpatrick

October 3, 1940, Daniel Fitzpatrick

French *Lebensraum*

Authentic Greek Masterpiece (Circa 1940).

December 12, 1940, Daniel Fitzpatrick

December 23, 1940, Daniel Fitzpatrick

Bringing Benito the Morning Mail

Richter

"The purpose of the Spanish World Axis is to study and resolve the common spiritual and
material necessities of our race"

February 12, 1941,
Mischa Richter

"It's time for the attack—we will continue the game in a prison camp."

February 28, 1941,
Mischa Richter

"Him? That's the Doctor"

These men tried to do business with Hitler—and look at them now.

The New Fuehrer

November 23, 1941,
Dr. Seuss

December 17, 1941,
Dr. Seuss

"Please, Uncle Henri ... won't you
take this up with Santa?"

April 23, 1942, Dr. Seuss

May 8, 1942, Dr. Seuss

Saber Rattling (By Remote Control)

May 30, 1942, Dr. Seuss

Caesar and Cleopatra

July 6, 1942, Dr. Seuss

196

September 13, 1942, Saul Steinberg

September 16, 1942, Saul Steinberg

Warming Up the Springboard

"A bit more spring, please, und I'll show 'em a Suez Flip mit an Algerian Twist und a hooper-dooper Double Dakar-South Atlantic Finish!"

July 10, 1942, Dr. Seuss

September 4, 1942, Dr. Seuss

"Cheer up, boys! Your Congress is going to declare an all-out war . . . after those November elections."

Herr Laval

Piping the New Admiral Aboard

November 30, 1942, Dr. Seuss

December 2, 1942, Dr. Seuss

"Are your bags packed, Sir? They're exhibiting you in the Museum."

December 15, 1942, Dr. Seuss

December 31, 1942, Dr. Seuss

May 12, 1943, Eric Godal

"We must fall with honor and dignity." *(Sec. General Scorza)*

May 20, 1943, Eric Godal

The Italian Quiz Kids

May 26, 1943, Carl Rose

205

Petain: "Tie me well, Adolf, and use some obvious violence.
I'll be able to say it was coercion."

'Everything except 'Fraternite'

July 18, 1943,
Eric Godal

The Forgotten Man?

July 26, 1943,
Eric Godal

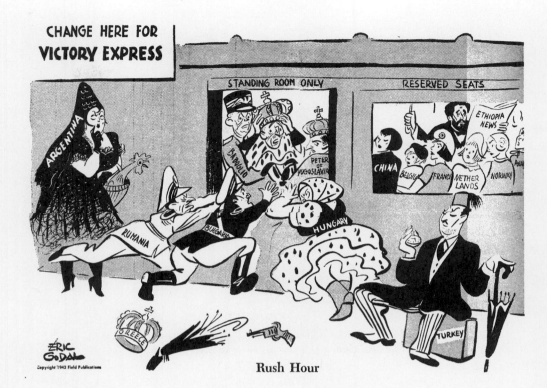

November 9, 1943,
Eric Godal

Rush Hour

January 28, 1944,
Eric Godal

News Item: Fascist Spain complains of Allied war of nerves.

February 21, 1944,
Eric Godal

"I have the grave duty to inform you that we lost one of our most distinguished members,
a man who succeeded in betraying two countries at once."

February 6, 1944,
Eric Godal

"Dusting's not enough. The boss ought to throw out the whole caboodle!"

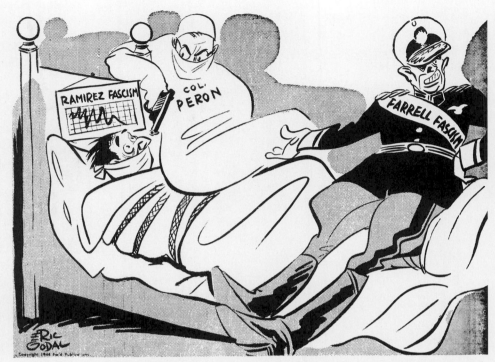

March 6, 1944,
Eric Godal

"We only run Argentina for poor sick Ramirez until he has a chance to recover."

March 20, 1944,
Eric Godal

March 16, 1944, Arthur Szyk

"Poor De Valera"

(Copyright, 1944, by Field Publications)

213

"Don't look at the record. Look at him!"

Appeasement for Appeasers

'No, No, Ivan — You Can't Kill Him — He's Mine!'

November 19, 1944, Melville Bernstein

"Just preparing for Summer vacations — mon General."

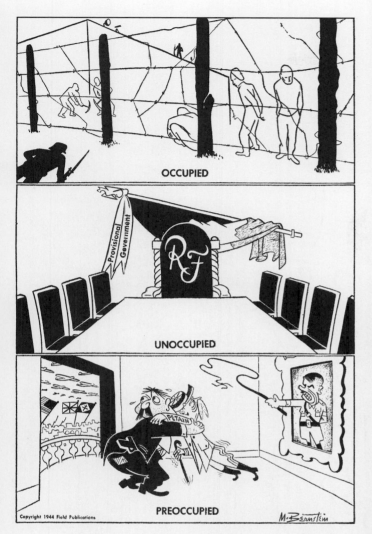

October 25, 1944, Eric Godal

June 18, 1944, Melville Bernstein

November 20, 1944,
Melville Bernstein

December 17, 1944,
Melville Bernstein

"... and the little mug on the end, too!"

The Inside Dope

Toward the Allied Victory
and the End of the War

With the Russian victory at Stalingrad, where the German army of 250,000 men was destroyed, *PM*'s relentless optimism seems more justified. Given the fears that *PM*'s readers must have felt at the start of the war, the cartoons it ran are largely celebratory and triumphalist. The images are overwhelmingly of Hitler facing defeat; relatively few appear about the Japanese. The war in Europe was far more immediate to the readers of *PM*, many of whose families came from there rather than from Asia. The one exception to the celebratory tone was the gradual realization of the Holocaust, though very partial at first, as has been discussed.

The other very real Allied difficulties, as in the invasion of Italy or the Battle of the Bulge, Germany's successful counterattack in 1944, are simply not mentioned. Nor are the political differences among the Allies. Issues like the British and French determination to maintain their empires after the war in opposition to Roosevelt's anticolonialist stance, questions which should have been of interest to *PM*, are not subjects of cartoons. Nor are the disagreements with Russia, though these are obliquely papered over with cartoons celebrating the meetings of the Big Three or the glories of the Russian army and the benefits of the American alliance with their forces.

Only occasionally do we see a cartoon referring to disagreement within the United States. In an editorial of August 1943, headlined "Don't Let the News Sell Out Our Dead," with an illustrative cartoon by the omnipresent Eric Godal, we see a strong statement by Victor H. Bernstein, who wrote many of the opinion pieces about foreign affairs. He cites an editorial in the

Daily News, PM's favorite local enemy (itself the butt of many cartoons, such as Seuss's of May 1, 1942), in which that paper questions the principle of unconditional surrender, "at almost precisely the moment when Berlin radio and every pro-Fascist and crackpot organization are doing the same thing." The *News* goes on to argue that a separate peace would save many lives, German and American. But Bernstein insists on finding the real reason for the editorial: not a hope that the German people will rise in revolt against their Nazi masters, but the fear that their ultimate surrender will put the Russians in a position to install their own, communist government. In other words, to "turn the war against fascism into one against communism." Bernstein ends by hoping that a free Germany will become a democratic one, but we see again the battle mentioned earlier between those who welcomed the alliance with Russia and those who, all along, had hoped to do without it.

On October 28, 1943, Max Lerner attacks another potential postwar danger; Lerner was one of *PM*'s most frequent and acute commentators. Here he attacks the proposal by the conservative Senators Connally and Vanderbergh that he argues would prevent the United States from joining any postwar international organizations. Far from making an isolationist America safer, he argues that it would force America to fight future wars on its own, leading to a militarized and ultimately Fascist country. (Lerner did not guess that America might join the U.N. and still see many of his fears materialize.)

On January 18, 1944, *PM* ran another editorial by its editor John P. Lewis on the fears of a separate peace.

It was a careful analysis of an article in *Pravda* dissecting reported British secret contacts with Ribbentrop to consider a separate peace. Clearly this was a major Soviet worry, but *PM* subtly suggests that this report is basically a red herring. Russia is trying to warn the West away from meddling in its plans for Poland and in further delaying its invasion of Western Europe. It may be "the Soviets' inept way of saying no Darlan deals in Germany." *PM* is still smarting over Roosevelt's decisions in North Africa. American lives may have been saved by the deal with Vichy, but America's commitment to unconditional surrender had been placed in doubt by American liberals, not to mention the Russians themselves.

As if to reinforce its patriotic and bellicose stance, *PM* continued to glory in the effectiveness of American bombing raids, not just in Japan but in Germany. The cartoon of March 9, 1944, recalls Seuss's attack on John Haynes Homes, the Protestant pastor who called the Japanese his brothers. Here the target is anyone protesting the ever more powerful—and increasingly unnecessary—bombings of German cities. The timing suggests that the protests may have followed the notorious bombing of Dresden on February 13–14, under the direction of "Bomber" Harris, the British general who had begun his career bombing Iraqi civilians in the 1920s. The approaching Russian armies had not requested the bombardment of this beautiful and now overcrowded city. The industrial targets were barely hit, and as many as 135,000 people may have been killed, to no military advantage.[15] But *PM* neither knew nor cared about these details.

As the German defeat seemed ever closer, *PM* concentrated more on the postwar era. We see an increasing number of cartoons on punishing war crimes. The attacks on the economic cartels also grow (see pages 103 and 263), along with the fear that their former American partners will somehow recreate the pre-war alliances that *PM* had so opposed. Finally, more attention is paid to continuing the New Deal after the war. In November 1943, *PM* would front-page the proposals of Walter Reuther, the dynamic and progressive leader of the car workers, UAW, who would propose an extension of Roosevelt's early economic policies toward something resembling the social democracy that Europe would turn to after the war.

PM's unabashed populist optimism is shown in Godal's cartoon on page 242 (from December 8, 1943), showing the "common man" directing the big four's "victory symphony," an image blissfully ignorant of the power struggles going on among them and their relative lack of concern for *PM*'s postwar agenda.

However, Bernstein's full-page drawing on page 250 (from February 18, 1944) shows that *PM*'s enemies have not been forgotten. Goebbels is shown giving a medal to the newspapers *PM* opposed. In addition to Hitler's allies, we see Father Coughlin; Lindbergh; Congressman Rankin, one of the worst of the Southern racists and anti-Semites; and Fritz Kuhn, the leader of the long-forgotten German American Bund, all sharing the same family tree.

On page 255, *PM*'s cartoonists refer to the failed generals' plot on July 20, 1944, which nearly killed Hitler and would have sparked a military revolt against him. They were soon tried and executed in the most painful manner possible, but the cartoons show neither support nor sympathy for this admittedly belated attempt.

On page 264 (from May 17, 1945), a delightful Steinberg cartoon, his last for *PM*, shows Hitler suggesting we all forget the past, something that *PM* would try to prevent the American public from doing as the concentration camps are open and the battle over Jewish emigration to Palestine begins.

February 4, 1943, Saul Steinberg

228

"So sorry—I have nothing to offer but blood, sweat, tears, evacuation, and Hon. Hara Kiri!"

INSIDE GERMANY   by Godal

May 9, 1943, Eric Godal

"How do we report this? The R.A.F.—enemy agents—or, the Gods forbid, sabotage?"

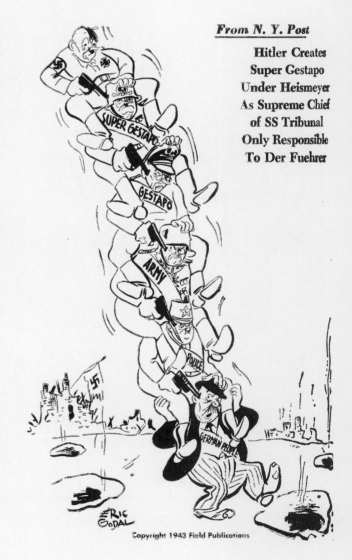

From N. Y. Post

Hitler Creates Super Gestapo Under Heismeyer As Supreme Chief of SS Tribunal Only Responsible To Der Fuehrer

May 28, 1943, Eric Godal

230

FUEHRER AND FEWER (*The Fuehrer Principle*)

To be shot as dangerous enemies of the Third Reich!

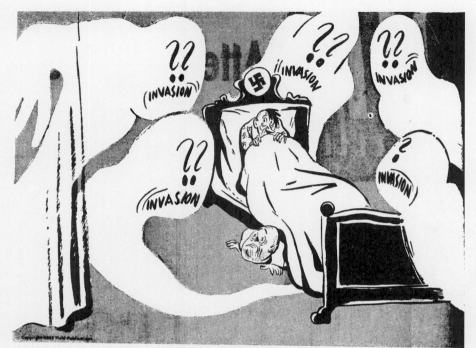

June 9, 1943, Eric Godal

"Pleasant Nightmares, Gentlemen!"

July 15, 1943, Eric Godal

"Gentlemen—You May Go Now. We Are Taking Over Again!"

"Who sang 'We Are Failing Against England'?"

June 27, 1943, Eric Godal

July 27, 1943, Eric Godal

"Adolf—Time passes so quickly!"

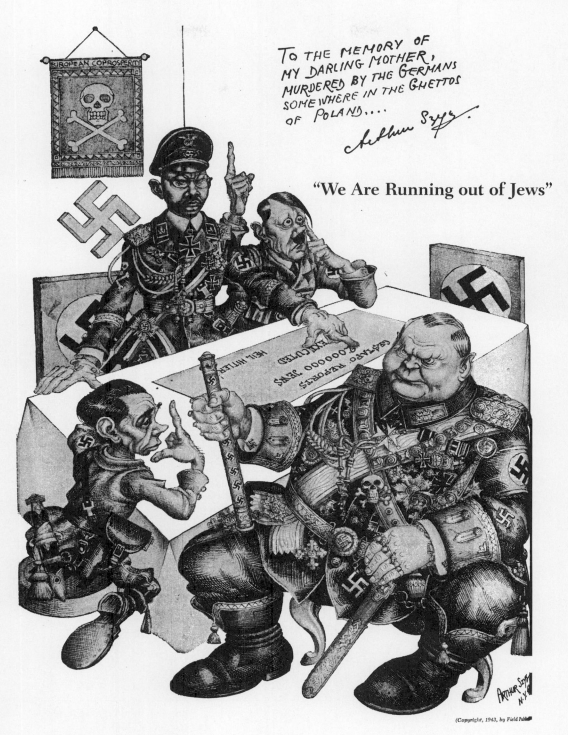

235

September 1, 1943,
Eric Godal

August 22, 1943,
Melville Bernstein

"Are you thinking what I'm thinking, General?"

By Bern

September 13, 1943, Melville Bernstein

WAR VOCABULARY (Revised)

By Melville Bernstein

Siegfried Line

Defense in Depth

Liquidation

Hitler's Timetable

Nazi Occupation

SS Troops

Motorized

Tomorrow the World

'The Rising Tide'

September 3, 1943,
Eric Godal

"German people—rest assured that no power on earth can block our retreat on the Russian Front!"

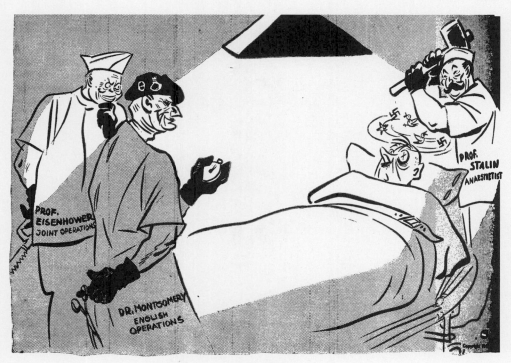

September 28, 1943,
Eric Godal

NOW?

"Here I am and here I will remain."—Hitler at the Dnieper.

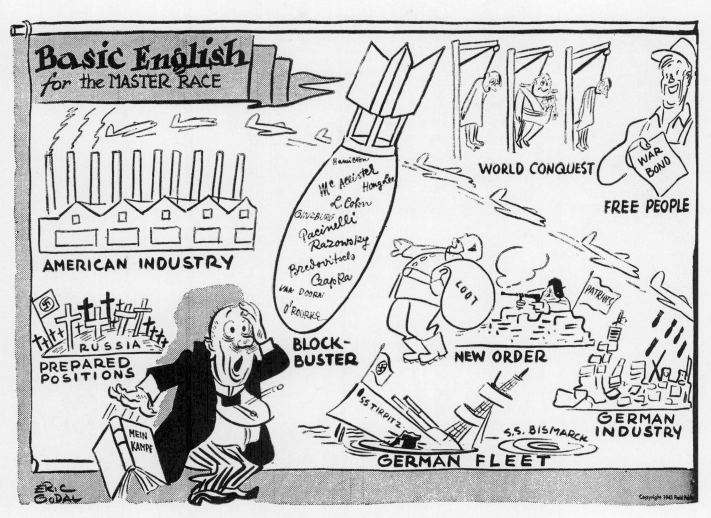

"Himmel! I didn't know it was so easy to understand!"

"And in the center will be the Victory Hall—monumental—colossal—gigantic—and
covered all over with pictures of myself!"

Last Rehearsals for the "Victory Symphony"

November 30, 1943,
Eric Godal

"Old stuff, Adolf—but it gives our appeasers something to work on!"

December 1, 1943,
Eric Godal

"Don't bother us now — we're just preparing for the next war!"

Radio Berlin: "The results of the talks among Churchill, Roosevelt, and Stalin are awaited here with complete calm"

December 2, 1943,
Eric Godal

December 20, 1943,
Eric Godal

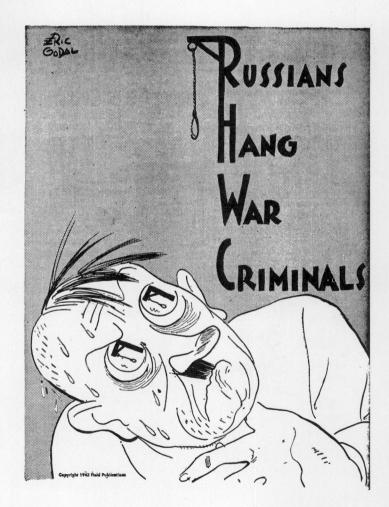

"Europe is getitng hot! We've got to move to the Western Hemisphere . . ."

***Hirohito*: "I am just another victim of Hitler—I thought he was winning . . . "**

"So Sorry! 'Tis the Will of the Emperor."

"How's Business, Partner?"

February 17, 1944,
Eric Godal

"Oh those American barbarians! Destroying my beautful ancient place of worship!"

February 22, 1944,
Eric Godal

"You still in the market for scrap iron, Tojo?"

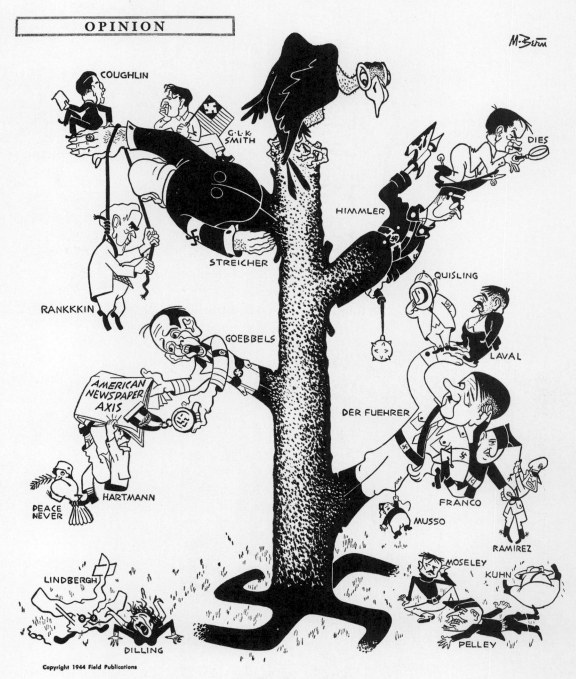

Family Tree

March 9, 1944,
Eric Godal

"Thanks Wotan — there are still some soft Americans left!"

May 22, 1944,
Eric Godal

"Mein Fuehrer—*Our* Invasion Is On!"

"Adolf — the Jig Is Up!'

July 10, 1944,
Eric Godal

NEWS ITEM: Hitler Has Taken Personal Command on the Western Front

July 26, 1944,
Eric Godal

German Soldiers Double Up on Hitler's Salute Order

September 4, 1944,
Eric Godal

Hour of Decision

September 7, 1944,
Eric Godal

"You Can Quit, Goebbels, That's the Man I Want!"

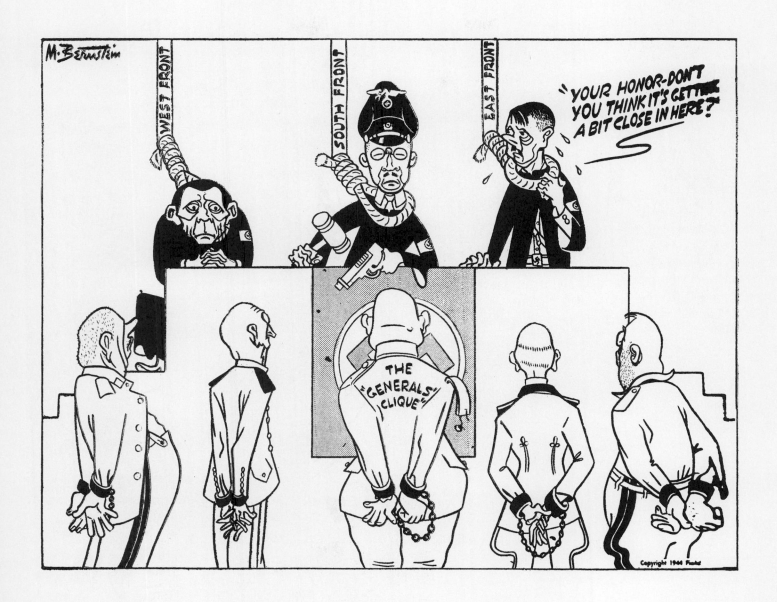

"I don't know what has come over me that I am so gloomy today."

A Fourth for Bridge

November 27, 1944, Eric Godal

'Who, Me?'

September 29, 1944,
Eric Godal

Last-Ditch Defense

October 20, 1944,
Eric Godal

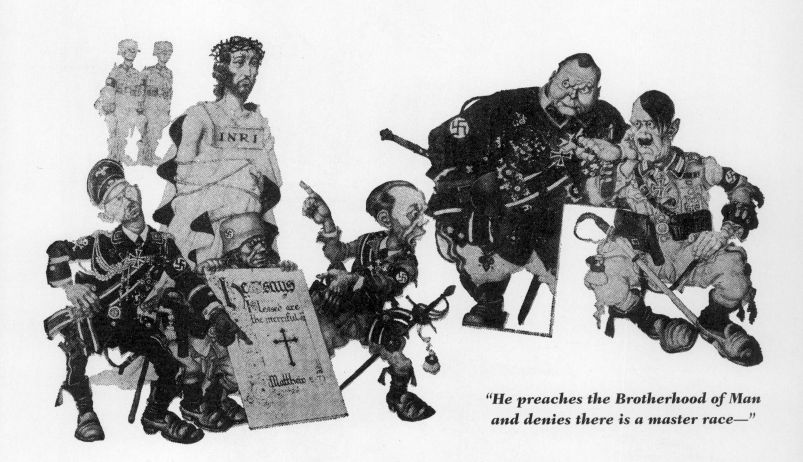

"He preaches the Brotherhood of Man
and denies there is a master race—"

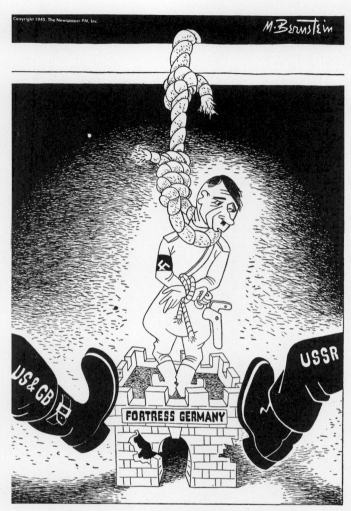

M. Bernstein

US & GB

USSR

FORTRESS GERMANY

Wait, gentlemen! Is this your considered opinion?

February 18, 1945,
Melville Bernstein

March 13, 1945,
Eric Godal

IMPERIAL PALACE

KEEP OUT!

Co-Prosperity Sphere

March 28, 1945,
Eric Godal

**"We Never Did Anything Real Bad to the Russians, but It Would Be Outrageous
If We—a Civilized People—Should BeTreated the Same Way."**

April 10, 1945,
Melville Bernstein

"Look, the Americans!
They've Come to Attack
Russia at last!"

". . . But We Still Hold the Initiative—We Can Surrender Any Time We Want"

August 8, 1945,
Melville Bernstein

August 9, 1945,
Melville Bernstein

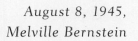

The Old One-Two

Acknowledgments

This volume owes its very existence to Richard Minear. His *Dr. Seuss Goes to War* opened up this field and showed America how powerful—and funny—Dr. Seuss's *PM* cartoons had been. Minear had photocopied thousand of pages that he did not use for *Dr. Seuss Goes to War* and had decided, in spite of our entreaties, that other scholarly commitments prevented him from making further use of these. In turning them over to us, he made available the treasure trove of material at the heart of this book. We are very grateful to him both for his industry and his generosity.

Many thanks to Lynda Claassen and Matthew Peters at the Mandeville Special Collections Library of the University of California, San Diego, for their important help in scanning the images of *PM* cartoons used in this volume. Additional thanks to Stewart Cauley, who retouched these digital scans with great care.

At The New Press, the preparation of this volume was greatly helped by Jyothi Natarajan, both in the gathering of the material and in the editing of the text. Her help was essential. The historian Lloyd Gardner kindly read through my text and kept me from making several mistakes, for which I am very grateful.

I am also grateful to Rebekah Heacock for her research on the microfilms of *PM*, now at the Tamiment Institute Library at NYU. Thanks as well to Frederick Wertheim for help in obtaining microfilm of past issues of *PM*.

My older daughter, Anya Schiffrin, who wrote her undergraduate thesis on *PM* and organized a conference of *PM* alumni at Tamiment, also gave valued advice.

Additional Reading

The crucial part of this book comes, of course, from the pages of *PM* itself. There is surprisingly little available on the history of this fascinating newspaper. The only book is *PM: A New Deal in Journalism, 1940–1948*, by Paul Milkman (New Brunswick: Rutgers University Press, 1997). In spite of its origins as a PhD thesis under Warren Sussman, it is a very enjoyable and fascinating book.

The one biography of Ralph Ingersoll, by Roy Hoopes, concentrates more on Ingersoll's very varied life and less on *PM*, though it contains some helpful information. There are a number of theses, including that by Anya Schiffrin, mentioned earlier, which concentrate on the paper's internal political battles, using interviews with several former staff members.

The literature on World War II and on American politics of this period is overwhelming. I will not attempt a full bibliography but will mention only those books that I have cited directly.

Blum, John Morton, *Liberty, Justice, Order* (New York: W.W. Norton & Co., Inc., 1993).

Calvocoressi, Peter, and Guy Wint, *Total War* (New York: Viking, 1972, 1989).

Davis, Kenneth S., *F.D.R.: The War President, 1940–1943* (New York: Random House, 2000).

Freidel, Frank, *America in the Twentieth Century* (New York: Alfred A. Knopf, 1965).

———, *Franklin D. Roosevelt: A Rendezvous with Destiny* (Boston: Little, Brown and Company, 1990).

Hoopes, Roy, *Ralph Ingersoll: A Biography* (New York: Atheneum Books, 1985).

Link, Arthur, and William Catton, *American Epoch: A History of the United States Since the 1890s* (New York: Alfred A. Knopf, 1967).

Preston, Paul, *Franco: A Biography* (New York: Basic Books, 1994).

Wyman, David, *The Abandonment of the Jews* (New York: Pantheon, 1985).

The information on newspaper cartoons about the Holocaust, other than *PM*'s, come from the Web site of the David Wyman Institute: htttp://www.wymaninstitute.org.

Some of the information in these pages is based on my own recollections or on conversations with individuals cited. I alone am responsible for these as well as any mistakes that may have escaped the attention of early readers and copy editors.

Notes

1. Paul Milkman, *PM: A New Deal in Journalism, 1940–1948* (New Brunswick: Rutgers University Press, 1997), 8.
2. Ibid., 23.
3. Kenneth S. Davis, *F.D.R.: The War President, 1940–1943* (New York: Random House, 2000), 286.
4. Ibid., 286.
5. David Wyman, *The Abandonment of the Jews: America and the Holocaust, 1941–1945* (New York: Pantheon, 1985), 15.
6. Frank Freidel, *America in the Twentieth Century* (New York: Alfred A. Knopf, 1965), 313.
7. John Morton Blum, *Liberty, Justice, Order* (New York: W.W. Norton & Co., Inc., 1993), 217.
8. Ibid., 217.
9. Richard H. Minear, *Dr. Seuss Goes to War: The World War II Editorial Cartoons of Theodor Seuss Geisel* (New York: The New Press, 1999), 184–185.
10. Wyman, 147.
11. Ibid., 15.
12. Freidel, 594.
13. Ibid., 377.
14. Ibid., 461.
15. Peter Calvocoressi and Guy Wint, *Total War* (New York: Viking, 1972, 1989), 562.

Chronological List of
Editorial Cartoons in This Volume